Sculpting Words: Carving Your Path to Masterful Writing

Perry L. Davidson

Published by Perry L. Davidson, 2024.

While every precaution has been taken in the preparation of this book, the publisher assumes no responsibility for errors or omissions, or for damages resulting from the use of the information contained herein.

SCULPTING WORDS: CARVING YOUR PATH TO MASTERFUL WRITING

First edition. November 8, 2024.

Copyright © 2024 Perry L. Davidson.

ISBN: 979-8227075291

Written by Perry L. Davidson.

Table of Contents

Sculpting Words: Carving Your Path to Masterful Writing 1

Preface 2

Chapter 1: Ditch the Data: The Power of Limited Research 4

Chapter 2: Self-Made Scribe: Writing Mastery Without Formal Education 14

Chapter 3: Write, Repeat: Structured Practice for Effective Writing . 24

Chapter 4: Perfectly Imperfect: Embracing Iterative Editing 33

Chapter 5: Simplify to Amplify: Crafting Powerful Narratives 44

Chapter 6: Feedback is Your Friend: Constructive Criticism as a Tool for Refinement 54

Chapter 7: Digital Drafting: The Role of Technology in Modern Writing 64

Chapter 8: The Heart of the Matter: Keeping Your Core Idea Front and Center 74

Chapter 9: The Writing Journey: Cultivating Joy in Creative Expression 84

Chapter 10: Breaking Creative Shackles: Unlocking New Writing Possibilities 94

Epilogue 104

Dedication

To the writers and dreamers,

This book is dedicated to you, the brave souls who dare to transform thoughts into words and words into worlds. May you find the inspiration, guidance, and courage to carve your own unique path to masterful writing, and may your stories shine brightly for all to see.

Epigraph

"Writing is the painting of the voice." — **Voltaire.**

Sculpting Words: Carving Your Path to Masterful Writing

Master the Art of Refining Your Ideas into Unforgettable Narratives in Weeks, Not Years – Without the Clutter of Over-Research and Stylistic Overwhelm

Preface

―――

"**I**ƒ *I had asked people what they wanted, they would have said faster horses.*" — Henry Ford.

This quote, often attributed to Henry Ford, might need more context in a book about writing. However, it beautifully encapsulates the essence of innovation and the courage to transcend conventional boundaries—themes at the heart of *Sculpting Words*.

This book is crafted to guide you, the writer, through a journey of distilling your overflowing ideas into clear, impactful narratives without being ensnared by the common traps of over-research and stylistic overwhelm.

Writing is an art, and like all artists, writers often struggle with their tools—be it research, form, tone, or style. These elements, though crucial, can sometimes become barriers rather than enablers of creativity. Recognizing this struggle firsthand from my interactions with both aspiring and seasoned writers, I felt a strong urge to create a pathway that simplifies these complexities. I aim to help you focus on what truly matters: carving your unique ideas into unforgettable narratives.

Imagine a writer named Emily, who spent years tweaking and researching her novel, constantly feeling like it wasn't enough to meet the literary standards she set. Or John, who abandoned multiple projects halfway because the extensive planning and styling felt stifling rather than liberating. These are not just hypothetical scenarios—they reflect fundamental challenges many writers face. Such stories propelled me to write this book to liberate creative minds from the shackles of conventional writing processes.

The methodologies in this book are inspired by a wide range of sources, from modern technological tools that aid writing to timeless advice from literary masters. The support and insights from various writing communities have been instrumental in shaping this guide. Their shared experiences and struggles highlight the need for a streamlined approach to writing—one that this book aims to fulfill.

By delving into these pages, you have taken a significant step toward transforming your writing process. This book is designed for writers like you, eager to break free from the clutter and focus on refining their craft. Prerequisite knowledge is optional except for a passion for writing and a willingness to embrace new techniques.

As you embark on this journey with me, remember that each page is a step toward mastering the art of writing with clarity and creativity. Your commitment to exploring these strategies is commendable and a vital part of your growth as a writer. I am deeply grateful for your trust and engagement in this shared adventure of learning and creativity.

So, thank you for choosing this guide. I invite you now to turn the page and begin sculpting your words into the stories only you can tell. Here's to finding clarity and joy in your writing journey—may the chapters ahead be as transformative as they are enlightening.

Chapter 1: Ditch the Data: The Power of Limited Research

Can Limiting Research Truly Sharpen a Writer's Focus?

Amelia sat at her old oak desk, the morning light spilling through the window and casting long shadows across the scattered papers and books. Her fingers hovered over the keyboard, poised yet hesitant. The room was silent except for the soft tapping of a branch against the window pane, a rhythmic reminder of the world outside her writer's den.

She had been here since dawn, chasing the tail of an idea for her novel that seemed to slip further away with each hour spent digging through historical accounts and literary critiques. The more she read, the more her words seemed to fade into obscurity, diluted by the vast ocean of information at her fingertips.

A gust of wind shook the window, drawing Amelia's gaze to a pair of robins flitting about in the garden. Their simple, purposeful movements struck a chord in her. Here they were, building a nest with no guide but instinct—a sharp contrast to her current state, buried under piles of research that felt more like shackles than aids.

She recalled an article she had skimmed weeks ago about setting research boundaries to enhance writing clarity and focus. The notion had seemed counterintuitive then; knowledge was power, after all. Yet now, as she watched those birds wield twigs with such decisive ease, Amelia wondered if there was wisdom in limitation.

The clock chimed ten times, pulling her back from thoughts of robins and research limits. She sighed and closed several browser tabs filled with academic jargon that clouded her plot rather than clarified it. Maybe it was time to try something different—set a timer for research or use software to block distractions.

Amelia pushed away from her desk and stepped outside for air. The garden was alive with mid-morning activity: bees buzzing around lavender bushes, leaves rustling softly underfoot, sunlight filtering through branches, creating patterns on the earth below. Each element existed not in isolation but as part of an intricate dance orchestrated by nature itself.

As she walked among this simplicity and orderliness, Amelia felt a shift within herself—a desire to emulate this natural economy in her writing process. Could imposing strict boundaries on research not only clarify her narrative but also reclaim hours lost down endless rabbit holes?

Does setting limits provide freedom from excess and guide us closer to our true intentions?

Unleash Your Creativity: Why Less Research Could Mean More Brilliance

In the realm of writing, there exists a common misconception that more research equates to better content. However, this opening chapter invites you to explore an intriguing counter perspective: could less be more regarding research? This notion might seem counterintuitive in an age where information is king and data is at our fingertips. Yet, there's compelling evidence that setting limits on research can sharpen your focus, enhance clarity, and elevate your writing.

The delicate balance between being well-informed and becoming inundated with information is at the heart of this discussion. Too often, writers fall into the rabbit hole of endless data gathering, mistaking accumulation for progress. This chapter aims to demystify the idea that extensive research is a prerequisite for excellent writing. Instead, it proposes that you can prevent common pitfalls such as procrastination and topic dilution by imposing strategic restrictions on research time and scope.

The Trap of Excessive Research

Understanding how excessive research can stifle creativity is crucial. It's easy to believe that immersing oneself in every possible detail will lead to a more prosperous composition. However, this approach can blur your main message and leave readers with unnecessary complexities. By recognizing the signs of over-researching, you can learn to pull back and refocus on what truly matters—your unique narrative voice.

Setting Boundaries: Techniques for Focused Research

Another vital skill this chapter addresses is learning techniques to set effective boundaries around your investigative process. Whether through technology that limits online browsing or methods for structuring your research time efficiently, these strategies are designed to keep your writing process under control. The goal is not just to manage time but to enhance the quality of your output by focusing on your core thesis.

Tools for Efficient Research

Exploring tools that aid in streamlining research will also be a key component of our discussion. These resources are invaluable, from digital applications that help organize notes to software solutions that block distracting websites during designated writing times.

They ensure that while you do conduct necessary research, it remains concise and does not impede the creative flow.

Navigating through these themes will not only optimize how you gather information but also transform how you think about the role of research in writing. By embracing a minimalist approach to data collection, you allow more room for creativity and personal insight to flourish.

This book, as a whole, seeks to guide writers through refining their ideas into polished narratives efficiently and enjoyably. By understanding the concepts laid out in this chapter, you'll begin a journey toward becoming a writer and a masterful sculptor of words—capable of transforming basic ideas into compelling stories with precision and flair.

Adopting these practices early on sets a foundation for all future chapters where we delve deeper into crafting unforgettable narratives without getting bogged down by over-research or stylistic overwhelm. As we progress through each section, remember: the essence of excellent writing lies not only in what you include but also in what you choose to leave out. Embrace simplicity in your research process, and watch your writing transform from cluttered thoughts into captivating tales.

Excessive research can be a double-edged sword for writers, often hindering rather than enhancing the creative process. While having a solid knowledge foundation before delving into a writing project is essential, too much information can lead to analysis paralysis and overwhelm. ***Spending countless hours immersed in research can divert focus from the core message*** one intends to convey, diluting the impact of the writing. It's crucial to balance gathering the necessary information and allowing space for original thoughts and ideas to flourish.

When writers get lost in the sea of data, they risk losing sight of their unique voice and perspective. The abundance of information available at our fingertips can be both a blessing and a curse. While it provides valuable insights and background for writing, it also presents the temptation to endlessly seek out more facts, figures, and opinions. This constant quest for more knowledge can create a barrier between the writer's authentic voice and the page, resulting in a piece that needs more clarity and conviction.

Moreover, excessive research can lead to procrastination, where writers continually postpone the actual writing process under the guise of *"further research."* This delay tactic hampers progress and diminishes the writer's confidence in their ability to articulate their ideas effectively. *The fear of not knowing enough can paralyze creativity,* preventing writers from taking risks and exploring innovative approaches to their work.

In essence, while research is an integral part of the writing process, *too much of it can stifle creativity.* Writers must learn to recognize when they've gathered enough information to support their ideas adequately and avoid getting lost in an endless cycle of data consumption. By setting boundaries and establishing clear goals for research, writers can reclaim their focus and unleash their creativity onto the page with clarity and purpose.

Ready to explore techniques to set boundaries for research and maintain focus?

Setting boundaries for research is crucial to maintaining focus and clarity in writing. **One effective technique** to limit research time is to **set specific time constraints.** By allocating a certain amount of time for research before starting to write, you prevent yourself from getting lost in an endless sea of information. Using **timers** or **setting alarms** can help you stay disciplined and ensure that you dedicate enough time to writing.

Another strategy is to **outline your main points before** delving into research. By having a clear structure in mind, you can tailor your research to only gather information relevant to your central ideas.

This prevents you from wandering off track and being sidetracked by exciting but ultimately unnecessary details. **Outlining** also serves as a roadmap, guiding you through the writing process and keeping your work focused.

Utilizing **research management tools** can also aid in setting boundaries. These tools can help you **block distracting websites**, limit internet usage during writing sessions, or even restrict access to specific sources that might lead you astray. Implementing these tools creates a controlled environment that promotes productivity and prevents the temptation to veer off course.

In addition to time constraints and outlining, it's essential to **establish clear goals** for your research. Define what specific information you need to support your main arguments or enhance your narrative. This targeted approach not only streamlines the research process but also ensures that every piece of information you gather strengthens your writing.

To further enforce boundaries, consider **working in a distraction-free environment**. Find a quiet space to focus solely on your writing without interruptions. This physical separation from potential distractions helps maintain your concentration. It allows you to dedicate your full attention to the task at hand.

Lastly, please don't underestimate the power of **self-discipline when** setting boundaries for research. Practice self-control by resisting the urge to veer off course during your writing sessions.

Remember the importance of staying focused and the benefits of producing concise, impactful work through limited research efforts.

By incorporating these techniques into your writing process, you can effectively set boundaries for research and ensure that your work remains clear, focused, and purposeful. *Quality* writing often stems from balancing thorough research and disciplined boundaries that prevent information overload.

In the quest for more focused and concise writing, exploring tools that help limit research time without sacrificing content quality can be a game-changer. These tools are designed to assist writers in staying on track with their research, preventing them from falling down endless internet rabbit holes. By utilizing these resources effectively, writers can harness the power of limited research to enhance the clarity and impact of their work.

One valuable tool for managing research time is the Pomodoro Technique. This method involves breaking work into intervals, typically 25 minutes long, separated by short breaks. During each interval, writers can dedicate their full attention to research tasks without distractions. By setting a timer and committing to focused research during these intervals, writers can make significant progress while ensuring they take necessary breaks to recharge.

Another helpful tool is website blockers, which can help writers avoid temptation and focus on their research goals. These blockers allow users to restrict access to distracting websites during designated work periods, enabling writers to maintain discipline and concentrate on gathering essential information for their writing projects.

Research management software is also instrumental in organizing and limiting research efforts. These programs enable writers to efficiently collect, categorize, and store relevant information. By centralizing research materials in one place, writers can easily access the needed data without getting lost in a sea of tabs or bookmarks.

Mind mapping tools offer a visual way to outline research findings and ideas. By creating a visual representation of the connections between different pieces of information, writers can clarify the structure of their work and ensure that all relevant points are included in their writing. This method can streamline research and help writers focus on their main arguments.

Setting specific goals for each research session is crucial in maintaining focus and avoiding unnecessary tangents. By defining what information needs to be gathered or what questions need to be answered before starting the research process, writers can stay on track and avoid getting sidetracked by irrelevant sources or details.

*Utilizing note-taking apps or software can help captu*re essential insights and key points during the research phase. These tools allow writers to record thoughts, quotes, and references efficiently, ensuring that valuable information is preserved and remembered as they progress.

Incorporating these tools into your writing process can help you navigate the sea of information available online with purpose and precision. By effectively leveraging these resources, you can balance thorough research and focused writing, ultimately producing more impactful and compelling content.

Embrace the Clarity of Limited Research

In our journey through this opening chapter, we've uncovered a vital truth: *less can indeed be more* regarding research in creative writing. The inclination to delve deeply into a sea of information can be strong, but as we've seen, setting limits is beneficial—it's essential for maintaining the clarity and focus of your writing.

By understanding the pitfalls of excessive research, you've equipped yourself with the knowledge to avoid common traps that lead to procrastination and the dilution of your core message.

Remember, your primary goal is to convey your ideas clearly and effectively, not to overwhelm your reader—or yourself—with excess data.

The techniques discussed for setting research boundaries, such as using timers or software that limits internet usage, are more than just tools; they are your allies in the creative process. They help preserve the essence of your narrative, ensuring that every piece of research serves the story rather than obscures it.

Moreover, the exploration of tools to limit research time is crucial.

These tools are not just about cutting down hours spent on research; they are about enhancing the quality of your content.

They ensure that every minute spent on research is purposeful and that every piece of information gathered drives your narrative forward.

Looking Ahead

As you progress into the following chapters, carry the lessons learned here. Let them guide you as you continue to refine your writing process. The path to masterful writing does not need to be cluttered with unnecessary detail. Instead, it should be paved with precision and purpose, leading you to craft narratives that resonate deeply with your readers.

This is just the beginning of our journey together. The strategies and insights we will explore in the coming chapters promise to further enhance your writing skills and confidence. By applying these principles, you are setting yourself on a course for improved writing and true mastery of the craft.

Embrace this process with enthusiasm and openness. The transformation you are about to experience in your writing will impact your work and touch your readers in profound ways. Here's to your success as you carve your path to becoming a masterful writer, one focused chapter at a time.

Chapter 2: Self-Made Scribe: Writing Mastery Without Formal Education

---

Can Passion Outweigh Formal Education in the Art of Writing?

Samuel found his sanctuary in the quiet hum of an old library, nestled in a small town where every face was familiar. The musty scent of aged paper mingled with the subtle creaks of wooden floors as patrons meandered through aisles lined with tales and truths. It was here, among these silent witnesses to history, that Samuel wrestled with his dreams.

He pulled a worn notebook from his bag—a faithful companion dotted with the scars of spilled thoughts. As he scribbled fervently, pausing now and then to gaze out the window at the fading sunlight, doubts whispered through his mind. The world seemed to insist on degrees and diplomas, credentials that hung on walls like trophies. But Samuel's walls were bare, adorned only with shadows and the occasional drawing from his niece.

A gentle breeze stirred the leaves outside, breaking his train of thought. He remembered stories of writers who had carved their paths without a formal guide, armed only with relentless passion and persistent practice. These tales were his beacon; they suggested a different kind of mastery—one forged in the fires of personal endeavor rather than structured schooling.

Across the room, Mrs. Ellington shuffled through her cart of books, each step echoing softly. Her presence was comforting—a reminder that stories weren't just written on pages but were lived by those who walked among these shelves. She had once told him that every book was a life unto itself; perhaps every writer's journey was, too.

Samuel closed his eyes briefly, letting the symphony of rustling pages and distant footsteps fill him with resolve. The sun dipped lower, casting long shadows that danced across his page. He imagined future days filled not with certificates but with pages inked by his hand—stories that spoke of human experiences as raw and honest as the ones he witnessed in this room.

As he packed away his notebook, leaving behind a trail of half-formed characters longing for their next breath on paper, he pondered whether it was indeed possible for sheer passion to match the accolades earned through formal education in writing?

What do you think—can personal dedication truly rival academic achievement in mastering an art?

Can You Become a Master Writer Without a Degree?

The conventional wisdom insists that a formal education is the gateway to mastering any craft, mainly writing. However, the truth often diverges sharply from this well-trodden path. The journey to becoming a self-made scribe is less about the credentials one acquires and more about the passion, dedication, and resilience one brings. This chapter dismantles long-held myths about the prerequisites for writing success. It offers a fresh perspective on forging your path in the literary world.

The Myth of Formal Education

For decades, aspiring writers have been funneled toward university degrees and writing workshops, with the promise that these are necessary stepping stones to literary excellence. Yet, history and present-day realities teem with writers who have carved their niches without formal trappings. These individuals underscore a powerful point: **mastery in writing isn't confined to lecture halls.** Instead, it blooms wherever there is a relentless pursuit of knowledge and an unwavering commitment to craft.

Crafting Your Own Curriculum

In today's digital age, resources for learning and improvement are boundless. A self-directed learner can access online courses, workshops, and a global community of writers at the click of a button. This chapter will explore how you can design your own curriculum tailored to your specific writing goals. This personalized learning approach allows for flexibility and adaptation that traditional educational structures often lack, enabling you to focus intensely on refining your unique voice.

The Power of Persistence

Passion and *persistence* are the most critical components of any writer's toolbox. The journey of a self-taught writer is punctuated by trials and errors, successes and failures. Each setback is an opportunity to learn, and each victory is a chance to improve. This chapter emphasizes that continuous practice is about frequently writing, reflecting critically on your work, and learning from others.

Cultivating Your Unique Voice

Every great writer has a distinct voice—an expression unique to their personality and experiences. Developing this voice requires reading extensively, writing incessantly, and having the courage to let your true self seep through your words. Here, we will discuss strategies to help you express your authentic self through your writing, which is essential in connecting deeply with your readers.

The essence of mastering writing through self-education lies in recognizing that *the most potent lessons are those learned in pursuing a passion*. As you navigate this chapter, remember that every word you write adds a stroke to your portrait as an author. By debunking outdated myths, embracing continuous learning, persisting through challenges, and nurturing your unique voice, you can achieve mastery in writing on your own terms.

This exploration isn't just about rejecting formal education and empowering you to take control of your literary journey. With each page turned, let's redefine what it means to be a masterful writer in an ever-evolving world.

Many aspiring writers believe that formal education is a prerequisite for success in the writing world. They feel more adequate with a degree or certification in creative writing or literature. However, the truth is that *mastery in writing does not necessarily require formal training*. Countless successful authors have achieved literary acclaim without the backing of a traditional education. The misconception that formal schooling is essential for becoming a skilled writer can hinder many from pursuing their passion.

Passion**,** *practice, and perseverance* are the cornerstones of becoming a proficient writer. While formal education can provide valuable guidance and structure, there are other paths to mastering the craft of writing. Self-taught writers often bring a unique perspective and voice to their work, unencumbered by academic conventions. Their journey to success is paved with dedication to honing their skills through continuous practice and unwavering commitment to their craft.

Embracing the idea that *writing mastery can be achieved without formal education* opens up a world of possibilities for aspiring writers. It shifts the focus from feeling inadequate without academic credentials to recognizing the power of individual creativity and determination. By understanding that one's passion for writing and consistent effort are the keys to success, writers can liberate themselves from the constraints of conventional wisdom.

Unveiling this truth allows writers to break free from self-imposed limitations and embrace their unique journey toward mastering the art of storytelling.

Discovering effective strategies to self-educate and continuously practice writing is crucial for aspiring writers aiming to master their craft. *One key strategy* is immersing oneself in various genres and styles, absorbing different techniques and approaches. By dissecting the works of established authors, aspiring writers can gain valuable insights into storytelling, character development, plot structuring, and language use. This continual exposure to diverse writing styles helps in shaping one's own unique voice and honing one's skills through observation and emulation.

Another vital strategy is setting aside dedicated time for regular writing practice. Consistent practice helps improve technical skills, nurtures creativity, and boosts confidence. Whether it's daily journaling, working on short stories, or experimenting with different forms of writing, the key is to make writing a habit. Like any other skill, writing requires consistent effort and practice to see tangible growth and development over time.

In addition, seeking feedback from peers or joining writing groups can provide valuable perspectives on one's work. Constructive criticism and encouragement from fellow writers can offer fresh insights, point out blind spots, and motivate individuals to push their boundaries. Engaging in discussions about writing techniques, sharing experiences, and receiving feedback can foster a sense of community that fuels motivation and learning.

Moreover, embracing online resources such as writing workshops, webinars, podcasts, and online courses can offer structured guidance and expert advice on various aspects of writing. These resources provide convenient avenues for self-education, allowing writers to learn at their own pace and explore specific areas of interest or improvement. Leveraging these digital platforms can enhance knowledge, offer practical tips, and keep writers inspired on their learning journey.

Furthermore, creating a conducive writing environment that sparks creativity and focus is essential for productive practice sessions. Whether setting up a cozy corner with inspiring decor, using tools like noise-canceling headphones or ambient music, or establishing a daily ritual before diving into writing, optimizing the workspace can significantly impact one's ability to concentrate and unleash creative energy.

Additionally, incorporating regular reflection sessions into the writing routine can help track progress, identify strengths and weaknesses, and set achievable goals for improvement. Self-assessment allows writers to evaluate their growth objectively, celebrate milestones, learn from setbacks, and adjust strategies accordingly to continue evolving in their craft.

Lastly, maintaining a growth mindset throughout the learning process is fundamental in overcoming challenges and embracing continuous improvement. By viewing setbacks as opportunities for learning rather than failures, writers can cultivate resilience, adaptability, and a positive attitude toward honing their skills.

Embracing a growth mindset fosters perseverance in the face of obstacles. It encourages a lifelong commitment to mastering the art of writing through dedication and passion.

By consistently integrating these strategies into their writing practice, aspiring writers can achieve significant growth, self-discovery, and mastery without the constraints of formal education.

Passion and persistence are the cornerstones of developing a unique writing voice. *Passion* fuels the writer, providing the drive to keep going when faced with challenges. The spark ignites creativity and pushes one to explore new ideas fearlessly. *On* the other hand, persistence is the unwavering commitment to the craft, showing up day after day to hone skills and refine one's voice. The backbone supports the writer through rejections, failures, and moments of self-doubt. Passion and persistence form a potent combination that propels writers toward mastery.

Finding your unique voice in writing is akin to discovering your fingerprint in a sea of impressions. **Embracing your uniqueness** is not about conforming to a standard but celebrating what sets you apart. Your experiences, perspectives, and emotions shape your voice, making it distinctively yours. By embracing this individuality, you infuse your writing with authenticity and resonance that captivates readers.

Developing a unique writing voice is not an overnight achievement but a continuous growth and evolution journey. **Practice, experimentation, and feedback** play vital roles in this process.

Regular practice hones your skills and refines your style. At the same time, experimentation allows you to push boundaries and discover new facets of your voice. Seeking feedback from trusted sources provides valuable insights that can guide your development and help you refine your unique tone.

To develop a unique writing voice, it's essential to **stay true to yourself**. Authenticity lies at the heart of compelling writing, resonating profoundly with readers. When you write from a place of honesty and vulnerability, your words carry an authenticity that connects with others authentically. Embrace your quirks, vulnerabilities, and idiosyncrasies in your writing; they are what make your voice distinctive.

Writing is as much about self-discovery as it is about storytelling. By honing your craft and developing your voice, you uncover layers of yourself that were previously unseen. *Self-reflection becomes* a powerful tool for growth, allowing you to delve deep into your thoughts and emotions, translating them into compelling narratives that resonate with others.

Ultimately, passion and persistence paved the way for writers to discover their unique path in the literary landscape. By embracing these qualities wholeheartedly, writers can transcend barriers imposed by formal education or external validation and create genuinely authentic and impactful works. The journey towards mastering writing without formal education begins with a deep-seated passion for storytelling and an unwavering commitment to honing one's craft - two pillars that sustain writers through every twist and turn on their path to mastery.

Embracing Your Journey as a Writer

The journey to becoming a masterful writer is often perceived as one that requires formal education and traditional pathways. However, the essence of writing is not confined within the walls of academia. It thrives in the passionate hearts and persistent efforts of those who dare to express themselves through words, regardless of their educational background.

Writing mastery is accessible to everyone. It is a craft honed by the relentless pursuit of self-improvement and the continuous practice of putting pen to paper. Every page you write adds another layer to your skill, and every revision sharpens your voice. The myths suggesting that only formally educated individuals can achieve writing success are just that—myths. They limit the vast potential that lies within self-directed learning and personal dedication.

The strategies for self-education in writing are numerous and varied. From reading widely and critically and engaging with a community of writers to experimenting with different styles and genres, your education as a writer is limited only by your willingness to explore and learn. The beauty of this journey lies in its flexibility and adaptability to your unique rhythm and life circumstances.

Passion and persistence are your most reliable allies. They fuel your motivation during challenging times and inspire you to refine your craft, even when progress seems slow. Your unique voice—your most valuable asset as a writer—will emerge not from following a prescribed path but from your authentic expression and the truths you share through your narratives.

Remember, every great writer was once a beginner who chose to take that first step: write that first word. Your path to writing mastery might be unconventional, but it is more valid and achievable. Embrace the freedom to learn and grow at your own pace, drawing from the rich experiences of both life and the imaginary worlds you create.

As you move forward, let your passion for storytelling guide you through the complexities of character arcs and plot twists. Let your persistence be the gentle but firm hand that keeps you anchored during storms of doubt or criticism. With each word you write, you are not just telling a story but also telling the world that you are a writer, self-made and proud.

Your writing journey is deeply personal yet universally resonant. It reflects a commitment to mastering a craft and understanding the human condition. As you continue this adventure, know that your voice, stories, and perspectives add invaluable color to the tapestry of human expression.

Embrace this path with confidence and curiosity, knowing that the tools for success are already within your grasp. Continue to learn, to write, and to dream boldly. After all, the world awaits the stories only you can tell.

Chapter 3: Write, Repeat: Structured Practice for Effective Writing

Can Discipline in Writing Forge a Master Storyteller?

In the soft haze of dawn, Julia sat by her modest oak desk, the window beside her framing the sleepy town of Crestwood. Her fingers hovered over the keyboard, each key a gateway to worlds she yearned to create. The blank document on her screen mirrored the empty streets outside—both waiting for life to stir within them. Today, like every day, she faced the vast sea of creativity and discipline that lay before her.

Her mind wandered back to last evening's writing group meeting where an older gentleman had shared his secret: *"Structured practice,"* he said with a voice smooth as worn leather, *"is key."*

Julia remembered how his eyes had sparkled as he spoke about setting daily word count goals and dedicating specific hours to writing, irrespective of the muses' whims. Inspired yet doubtful, she pondered if such rigor could be the scaffold upon which great narratives were built.

The clock ticked audibly in her quiet room, slicing through her reverie. She noticed a sparrow perched on her windowsill, pecking at crumbs from yesterday's breakfast. Its small life seemed governed by simple needs and routines. Perhaps there was merit in regularity, not just for survival but for flourishing.

She typed one word, then another, forming a sentence—a small commitment to this new discipline regime. Her coffee cooled in its mug as she wrote about characters who danced at the edges of her imagination. They were no longer shadows but beings with desires and fears, painted against the backdrop of worlds only she could construct.

As Julia's room brightened with morning light reflecting off her screen filled with words now teeming with life and conflict, she wondered if tomorrow she would look forward to this routine that today felt so foreign. Could these structured practices truly refine raw thoughts into polished narratives? Would this path lead her to become a writer and master storyteller?

From Routine to Remarkable: Unlocking the Power of Structured Writing Practice

When it comes to mastering the art of writing, *discipline overshadows* sporadic bursts of inspiration. This truth resonates across all forms of artistry; consistent practice is not just beneficial but essential. As we delve into the heart of enhancing writing skills through structured training, we embrace a methodology that transforms sporadic writers into prolific wordsmiths. This approach isn't about rigid schedules that stifle creativity but about creating a framework that invites it daily.

Structured practice in writing is akin to training muscles in the gym; you would only expect to lift heavier weights with consistent training and the proper techniques. Similarly, setting daily word count goals or dedicated writing hours isn't merely a challenge to your creativity but a scaffold that elevates your skill level. By committing to these practices, you ensure that your writing muscles are flexed and strengthened, ready to perform when inspiration strikes.

The effectiveness of this method lies in its simplicity and its challenge. It's straightforward. It demands nothing more than showing up and writing. Yet, it is challenging because it requires this commitment even when the muse is silent. This chapter explores how adopting daily practices can significantly enhance your writing skills. We look at how to set realistic and effective writing goals and how implementing structured schedules can lead not just to increased output but to an improvement in the quality of writing.

Daily practices are more than routines; they are commitments to your craft. Whether drafting a novel, scripting a screenplay, or composing poetry, regular writing sharpens your ability to express ideas clearly and creatively. It's about turning the intangible—a fleeting thought or a vague notion—into tangible narratives that resonate with readers.

Setting *realistic and practical goals* is crucial in this journey.

Goals are not just numbers but reflections of your ambition tempered with practicality. They motivate and guide but should be manageable. In this discussion, we will navigate setting achievable targets that stretch your capabilities without breaking your spirit.

Lastly, *structured schedules* serve as the backbone of consistent output. They transform erratic bursts of productivity into steady streams of workable content. A well-planned schedule respects your creative process while imposing enough discipline to prevent procrastination and creative blocks. It's about finding balance—structuring time so creativity can flow freely within set boundaries.

Through these practices, writers can achieve a harmony between discipline and inspiration. The goal is clear: to refine raw ideas into polished narratives efficiently and effectively. By embracing structured practice, writers do not just wait for inspiration but actively cultivate it daily.

This chapter promises to equip you with the tools needed for such transformation—turning potential into prowess through dedicated practice. As we proceed, remember that every word written is a step forward in your writing journey. Let us move forward together with purpose and passion.

Structured practice is the cornerstone of honing writing skills. By dedicating time each day to writing, individuals can steadily enhance their craft. Daily practices play a crucial role in developing a writer's voice, style, and proficiency. **Consistent writing routines** help foster discipline and creativity simultaneously. Writers who commit to regular writing sessions often find themselves more adept at translating their thoughts into compelling narratives.

Setting aside specific times for writing can be immensely beneficial. A designated writing schedule can boost productivity, whether early morning before the day starts, during lunch breaks, or in the quiet evening hours. *Establishing a routine helps* prepare the mind for creative output at set times each day. This consistency can lead to improved focus and flow during writing sessions.

Moreover, daily practices enable writers to explore different styles, genres, and themes regularly. *Variety in writing* keeps the creative juices flowing. It allows individuals to expand their skills and experiment with new forms of expression. Through consistent practice, writers can push their boundaries and discover hidden talents they might not have otherwise uncovered.

In addition to enhancing technical skills, daily writing practices also contribute to *building confidence* in one's abilities. The more frequently one engages with the writing process, the more comfortable and assured they become in their storytelling. Confidence is vital in overcoming self-doubt and hesitation that often plague writers, allowing them to take risks and explore bold ideas fearlessly.

Furthermore, daily writing routines foster a sense of commitment to one's craft. Individuals demonstrate their dedication to improving and growing as writers by showing up every day to write. This dedication translates into tangible progress over time, as small daily efforts accumulate into significant developments in skill and artistry.

Embark on this journey of structured practice and witness your writing skills flourish with each passing day.

Setting realistic and practical writing goals is crucial for honing your craft and progressing in your writing journey. *Establishing specific objectives* gives you a clear direction to work towards, keeping you focused and motivated. Setting *goals that are attainable* within your current schedule and skill level is essential.

Pushing yourself is vital for growth, but setting unachievable goals can lead to frustration and demotivation.

Consider breaking down your larger writing goals into smaller, manageable tasks. This approach allows you to track your progress more effectively and gives you a sense of accomplishment as you complete each task. *Setting daily or weekly word count targets* creates a structured framework to operate, ensuring steady progress over time. These bite-sized goals make the writing process less daunting and more achievable.

Another critical aspect of effective goal-setting is consistency. Establishing a routine for your writing practice helps cultivate discipline. It makes it easier to prioritize your creative work amidst other responsibilities. Whether dedicating a specific time of day to write or committing to a certain number of writing sessions per week, consistency is crucial in improving your skills.

Tracking your progress is essential when working towards your writing goals. Please keep a record of the milestones you reach, whether completing a chapter, meeting a word count target, or receiving positive feedback on your work. *This documentation motivates you by showcasing how far you've come* and provides valuable insights into your writing process and areas for improvement.

*Flexibility is also essential when setting writing goa*ls. While having a structured plan in place is beneficial, being open to adjustments based on feedback or evolving priorities can help you stay adaptable and responsive in your approach. *Be bold and tweak your goals if needed,* as long as the modifications align with your writing objectives.

Practical *writing goals should be specific, attainable, and consistent.* By breaking down larger objectives into smaller tasks, maintaining a routine, tracking progress, and staying flexible, you can set yourself up for success in your writing endeavors.

Remember that the journey towards mastering the art of writing is as much about the process as it is about the final destination.

Implementing a Structured Writing Model

A structured approach is crucial to enhancing writing skills effectively. This *"Process Model"* involves three key phases: planning, execution, and reflection. Each phase is vital in developing consistent writing habits and improving overall proficiency.

Planning Phase

In the planning phase, writers set clear and achievable goals for each writing session. This could include word count targets, specific sections to work on, or time blocks dedicated to writing.

Choosing a focused topic based on past reflections guides the writer in the right direction. The planning phase sets the foundation for productive writing sessions by providing a roadmap to follow.

Execution Phase

The execution phase is where the actual writing takes place.

Writers utilize timed sprints, creating distraction-free environments and using prompts to kickstart their writing process. Incorporating tools such as Pomodoro timers or apps that block distractions can help maintain focus during the writing session. This phase emphasizes the act of writing itself and overcoming any initial resistance to start.

Reflection Phase

The reflection phase is essential for growth and improvement. Writers review their work, identifying successes and areas for enhancement. This self-assessment can be complemented by seeking peer feedback or utilizing platforms that provide analytical insights into writing patterns. By documenting these reflections, writers can track progress and adjust their goals accordingly. The reflection phase closes the loop of continuous improvement in the writing process.

Dynamic Behavior of the Model

The model operates as a cyclical process, each phase feeding into the next in a continuous improvement loop. As writers progress through the model, they refine their skills, adapt their strategies, and become more proficient in their craft. The feedback loop created by reflection ensures that writers stay on track toward their goals while remaining open to adjustments based on their evolving needs.

Practical Implications

By following this structured process model, writers can develop disciplined yet flexible writing habits that lead to consistent output and skill enhancement. The model provides a framework for writers to approach their craft systematically, fostering growth and creativity sustainably. Through regular practice using this model, writers can see tangible improvements in their writing skills and overall productivity.

In summary, the *"Process Model"* of planning, execution, and reflection offers a practical framework for writers to effectively structure their daily writing routines. By incorporating this model into their practice, writers can cultivate discipline, foster growth, and enhance their writing skills over time with focused effort and dedication.

Pathway to Masterful Writing: A Step-by-Step Guide

Structured practice is the cornerstone of mastering any skill, and writing is no exception. By deliberately applying daily practices, realistic goal-setting, and structured schedules, you can elevate your writing from tentative experiments to polished narratives. This chapter focuses on equipping you with tools that foster consistent and effective writing habits.

Step 1: Explore daily practices that enhance writing skills. Setting aside a specific time each day for writing is crucial.

Consistency in your schedule and a conducive environment spark creativity and improve focus. Integrating varied writing exercises and reading broadly are equally important, as they refine your skills and expand your creative horizons.

Step 2: Set realistic and practical writing goals. Evaluate your current writing routine and then set specific, achievable objectives. Whether it's a word count, a page number, or a draft completion date, these goals should guide your daily writing efforts.

Prioritizing tasks and sticking to a schedule will help turn your aspirations into accomplishments.

Step 3: Implement structured schedules to promote consistent writing output. Use tools like writing journals or digital trackers to monitor your progress. Breaking your writing time into focused sessions can increase productivity and lessen fatigue. Establishing rituals also signals to your mind that it's time to write, aiding the transition into a creative state.

Remember, the pathway to improving your writing is about adhering to a rigid framework and allowing flexibility in your approach. Celebrate your milestones and learn from the setbacks. Each step forward in this journey is a building block in constructing your narrative artistry.

By embracing these structured practices, you're not just writing; you're sculpting your thoughts into clear, impactful narratives.

Keep this guide close, and let it lead you through the disciplined yet creative process of mastering the art of writing.

Chapter 4: Perfectly Imperfect: Embracing Iterative Editing

Can Iteration Unlock True Potential?

The sun hung low in the sky, casting elongated shadows that crept across the walls of Thomas's modest study. He sat hunched over his desk, papers strewn about like fallen leaves in autumn. Each sheet bore the scars of his relentless editing: scribbles, annotations, and the occasional coffee stain. The clock ticked steadily, a soft but constant reminder that time, unlike his drafts, never required revisions.

Thomas's mind wandered to his early days as a writer, when each word felt like a stone in a cathedral—permanent and significant.

Now, his approach had evolved; he understood the beauty in malleability. His latest project was a novel, one that seemed perpetually unfinished. Each chapter reflected not only the story he wanted to tell but also the person he was at each iteration.

Outside, a breeze stirred, sending a shiver through the open window and fluttering the pages on his desk. It whispered secrets only half-understood—much like how he felt about his writing process before adopting iterative editing. The method had taught him patience and resilience, qualities mirrored in the slow yet persistent growth of the oak tree just outside.

A knock at the door broke his concentration. Sarah, his neighbor and confidante in all things literary, stepped into the room with her usual quiet grace. *"Still wrestling with Chapter Seven?"* she asked with a knowing smile.

"Yes," Thomas sighed, *"but it's different now. I'm learning to listen more—to my characters and myself."* He shared how using tools like MovableType.ai had shifted his perspective on writing; it was less about chasing perfection from the start and more about evolving toward it.

They spoke of narrative clarity and impact—how each edited line didn't just bring him closer to an ideal manuscript and made him a better writer; feedback became less of critique and more of conversation with himself through different stages of creation.

As Sarah left, words of encouragement lingering in the air like the faint aroma of her herbal tea, Thomas turned back to his work with renewed vigor. The evening stretched before him, filled not with dread for deadlines but with possibilities within reach through refinement.

He pondered if every writer felt this transformation through iterative edits or if they still clung to old myths of perfect first drafts?

Why Strive for Perfection When Iteration Can Sculpt Mastery?

The journey of writing is often misconceived as a quest for immediate perfection. However, the artistry of writing, much like any form of creation, flourishes under continual refinement and revision. The notion that a writer must achieve perfection in the initial draft is daunting and impractical. Instead, embracing an iterative editing process can significantly enhance the quality and impact of your writing. This chapter explores how adopting a progressive approach to editing can transform good writing into great writing.

The Power of Iterative Editing

Understanding the benefits of iterative editing is fundamental to transforming your approach to writing. Initially, drafts are merely the raw clay from which your final masterpiece will emerge.

Revisiting and refining these drafts engages you in a dynamic process that sharpens your ideas and polishes your narrative. This method alleviates the pressure of achieving perfection on the first try. It opens up creative avenues that may not be apparent in a single pass.

Integrating Technology in Editing

In today's digital age, tools like MovableType.ai represent a pivotal shift in refining our drafts. These platforms provide objective feedback for improving your work's clarity and coherence. By incorporating such technology into your editing process, you gain insights that might take much longer to identify through traditional methods. This chapter will discuss how leveraging these tools can streamline the editing process and elevate the quality of your writing.

Techniques for Effective Phased Editing

Developing techniques for phased editing is essential for enhancing narrative clarity and ensuring that each element of your story aligns with your overall message. This approach allows you to focus intensely on different aspects of your text during various phases, from structural integrity to language finesse. By breaking down the editing process into manageable stages, you can concentrate on making incremental improvements that collectively boost the effectiveness of your narrative.

This chapter aims to shift your perspective from viewing editing as daunting to seeing it as an exciting opportunity for creative exploration. Through iterative editing, you learn about effective writing techniques and resilience and adaptability—qualities that define great writers.

Embrace the iterative process. Let go of the unattainable quest for first-draft perfection and welcome the growth that comes from revision. With each iteration, you will edge closer to articulating your thoughts more clearly and impactfully.

By understanding these principles and integrating sophisticated tools and structured techniques into your workflow, you are better equipped to sculpt words that resonate deeply with your readers.

Each section builds on this foundation, designed to guide you through mastering the art of iterative editing—turning promising ideas into polished narratives.

Ultimately, this chapter bridges the gap between where you are and where you aspire to be in your writing journey, empowering you with strategies that enhance both skill and confidence.

Iterative editing is a powerful ally in the writer's arsenal, offering a more practical approach to refining writing than the elusive quest for a flawless first draft. Rather than striving for perfection from the outset, embracing the iterative process allows writers to gradually enhance their work, shaping it into its best form over time. This method acknowledges that writing is a journey of refinement, with each edit bringing the narrative closer to its true potential. By focusing on incremental improvements, writers can avoid the overwhelming pressure of achieving perfection in one go and instead enjoy the gradual transformation of their work.

The beauty of iterative editing lies in its ability to unveil hidden gems within a piece of writing. Each round of edits reveals new layers, refines ideas, and clarifies the narrative, leading to a more polished final product. *This process allows writers to uncover nuances and subtleties that might have remained obscured in a rushed attempt at perfection.* By revisiting and revising their work multiple times, writers can delve deeper into their content, enhancing its richness and impact.

Moreover, iterative editing offers a practical advantage by streamlining the writing process. Instead of getting bogged down in pursuit of unattainable perfection in one go, writers can focus on gradual improvements that steadily elevate the quality of their work. *This approach saves time and fosters a sense of progression and growth throughout the editing journey.*

Critically, iterative editing nurtures resilience and flexibility in writers. It encourages them to embrace feedback, learn from mistakes, and adapt their writing based on insights gained during each iteration. *This adaptive mindset is essential for continuous improvement and development as a writer,* allowing for greater versatility in tackling diverse writing challenges.

Embrace the transformative power of iterative editing as we explore how digital tools like MovableType.ai can elevate your editing process.

Utilizing Digital Tools for Enhanced Writing

In writing, technology has become a valuable ally in the quest for improvement and efficiency. **Digital tools** like *MovableType.ai* offer writers a unique advantage by providing **objective feedback** and *suggestions* that can significantly enhance the editing process.

These tools act as virtual companions, offering insights and recommendations to help writers refine their work precisely and clearly.

MovableType.ai, in particular, stands out for its ability to analyze text comprehensively, pointing out areas for improvement in *grammar, style, and tone.* By leveraging such tools, writers can receive instant feedback on their drafts, enabling them to identify weak points and make necessary adjustments swiftly. This real-time assistance accelerates the editing process and serves as a guiding light toward crafting stronger narratives.

Integrating digital tools into the editing process revolutionizes how writers approach their craft. Instead of relying solely on personal judgment or sporadic feedback, these tools offer a consistent and reliable source of guidance. By embracing such technology, writers can hone their skills more effectively, moving closer to their desired level of mastery.

FEEDBACK LOOP FOR CONTINUOUS Improvement

One of the most significant advantages of utilizing digital tools like *MovableType.ai* is establishing a *feedback loop that* fosters continuous improvement. Through iterative editing guided by these tools, writers can address recurring issues in their writing, gradually enhancing the overall quality of their work.

The feedback loop created by digital tools enables writers to learn from their mistakes and refine their writing skills. By receiving targeted suggestions for improvement, writers can focus on specific areas that need enhancement, gradually elevating the quality of their content with each iteration.

Efficiency through Automation

In addition to providing valuable feedback, digital editing tools offer *automation* that streamlines the editing process. These tools swiftly handle tasks such as *grammar checks, style corrections*, and *formatting adjustments,* allowing writers to concentrate on higher-order aspects of their writing.

By automating routine editing tasks, writers can allocate more time and energy to refining the substance and structure of their work.

This efficiency accelerates the editing process and frees up mental bandwidth for creative exploration and strategic revisions.

Embracing Collaboration

Furthermore, digital tools facilitate *collaboration among* writers by enabling seamless sharing and review processes. Whether working on a team project or seeking peer input, these tools enhance communication and coordination, fostering community within the writing sphere.

Collaborative features within digital editing platforms empower writers to engage with others in a productive exchange of ideas and feedback. By leveraging these capabilities, writers can benefit from diverse perspectives and collective wisdom, enriching their writing journey with shared insights and experiences.

In conclusion, digital tools like *MovableType.ai* offer a powerful ally in the quest for enhanced writing. By embracing these technologies and incorporating them into the iterative editing process, writers can elevate their craft to new heights of excellence.

Through efficient feedback loops, automation benefits, and collaborative opportunities, these tools pave the way for continuous growth and improvement in the art of writing.

Developing techniques for phased editing is a crucial aspect of refining narrative clarity in writing. By breaking down the editing process into manageable phases, writers can focus on specific elements of their work at each stage, ensuring a more thorough and effective revision process. **Beginning with an overall assessment of the narrative structure and flow** allows writers to identify any inconsistencies or gaps in the storyline. This initial phase sets the foundation for subsequent edits, guiding the direction of the narrative toward greater coherence and impact.

Once the structural aspects are refined, attention can be turned towards enhancing character development and dialogue. *Delving deeper into characters' motivations and complexities helps* create more engaging and relatable personas within the story. Dialogue, when polished during this phase, can bring conversations to life, adding depth and authenticity to interactions between characters.

This focused approach to character development contributes significantly to the overall richness of the narrative.

The **next phase involves refining descriptive elements** within the writing. By paying close attention to sensory details, settings, and imagery, writers can create a vivid and immersive reading experience for their audience. *Utilizing evocative language* to paint scenes and evoke emotions enhances the overall impact of the narrative, drawing readers further into the world being crafted on the page.

The ***final phase centers on fine-tuning language and style*** as writers progress through these phased editing stages. This includes polishing grammar, syntax, word choice, and sentence structure to ensure clarity and precision in communication. *By meticulously reviewing each sentence for conciseness and effectiveness,* writers can elevate their prose to a higher level of refinement, enhancing readability and coherence throughout the piece.

Embracing phased editing allows for a systematic approach to refining writing. It fosters a deeper connection with the narrative being created. *Each phase builds upon the previous one,* culminating in a comprehensive revision process that elevates the quality of the work as a whole. By honing in on specific elements at different stages, writers can address critical areas of improvement methodically, leading to a more polished and impactful final draft.

In essence, **phased editing serves as a roadmap** for writers seeking to enhance narrative clarity in their work. *By dividing the editing process into distinct phases*, writers can navigate through revisions with purpose and precision, ultimately shaping their writing into a cohesive and compelling piece that resonates with readers. This structured approach not only streamlines the editing process but also empowers writers to refine their craft systematically, resulting in engaging and memorable narratives.

As we've discovered, iterative editing is not just a technique but a transformative approach that reshapes our understanding of the writing process. Embracing this method means accepting that our first drafts are merely the starting point—raw clay to be meticulously sculpted into something more refined and compelling. The journey from a rough draft to a polished piece involves multiple stages of revision, each aimed at enhancing different facets of the text.

Step 1: Dive into Iterative Editing

Start by acknowledging that perfection is unattainable on the first try and that your initial draft should act as a canvas to build. This mindset alleviates the pressure many writers feel to get everything right the first time and opens up a space for creative exploration. Each round of edits should focus on specific elements—be it narrative structure, character depth, or dialogue sharpness—allowing you to refine your story methodically.

Step 2: Leverage Digital Tools

Incorporate tools like MovableType.ai early in the editing process. These platforms use advanced algorithms to provide feedback that might be overlooked. By analyzing your work through these digital lenses, you can pinpoint areas that need tightening, thus making your narrative more transparent and engaging. Remember, these tools are here to supplement your editing prowess, not replace it.

Step 3: Phase Your Edits for Clarity

Begin with broad strokes, looking at your story's overall architecture for inconsistencies or narrative gaps. Once the larger picture is solid, focus on the finer details. This phased approach makes the task more manageable. It ensures that each element of your story—from plot progression to sentence structure—is polished.

Throughout these phases, keep the lines of communication open with peers or beta readers. Fresh eyes can offer invaluable perspectives and catch issues you might have missed. Contemplate their critiques and integrate feedback that aligns with your vision for the work.

This step-by-step process, *"Refine and Shine,"* is designed to enhance the quality of your writing and transform editing from a daunting task into an engaging part of your creative journey. It allows you to build resilience as a writer and instills a habit of continuous improvement. By breaking down editing into manageable phases and using tools to augment this process, you ensure that each piece you craft reaches its highest potential.

As we move forward, let's carry with us the understanding that our words are clay—malleable and ever-responsive to the artist's touch. With each pass over our work, we come closer to revealing the vivid stories that resonate deeply with our readers. Remember, the beauty of writing lies not in flawless first attempts but in our willingness to revise, reshape, and refine. This is how we sculpt narratives that endure.

Chapter 5: Simplify to Amplify: Crafting Powerful Narratives

Can Clarity Truly Captivate?

Lucas stood by the window, the morning light glowing warmly across his cluttered desk. Papers, filled with scribbles and edits, lay scattered like fallen leaves in autumn. He had been trying to write a novel that would grip readers with its clarity and brevity. Yet, he was tangled in a web of overcomplicated narratives and convoluted subplots. His fingers tapped rhythmically against the wooden frame, each tap echoing his mounting frustration.

Outside, the city was waking up; cars murmured along the streets, and distant voices merged into a low hum. Lucas watched as a young woman at the bus stop flipped through a book, her face alight with intrigue. He wondered what magic lay within those pages that held her so captivated. Turning back to his work, he felt a pang of envy – for her absorption in another's words and the simplicity he struggled to achieve in his writing.

As he resumed his seat, Lucas's mind wandered back to his college days when Professor Elm had lectured on the power of simplicity in storytelling. *"The strength of your story lies not in the complexity of its vocabulary or the intricacy of its plot twists,"* Elm had said, *"but in how deeply it can touch the reader's heart through simple truths."* Those words had inspired him once; now, they taunted him from memory.

He picked up one of his drafts and read aloud, trying to hear where he could strip away excess and reveal the story's true essence. With each sentence spoken into the stillness of his room, Lucas felt both judge and jury over his words. The story needed to breathe without being choked by unnecessary flourishes.

A soft knock on the door broke his concentration. It was Mrs. Collier from next door bringing him some fresh scones she had baked that morning. Her presence was a gentle reminder of life's simpler pleasures – an interruption that brought relief more than anything else.

"Thank you," Lucas smiled as he accepted her gesture with genuine gratitude.

Returning to his desk after she left, Lucas felt slightly lighter. Perhaps what he needed was not relentless revision but moments like these—reminders of life's unadorned joys that could translate into clear and powerful writing.

Why do we often complicate what we wish to express? Could our deepest fear be not being misunderstood but instead being too easily understood?

Less is More: Unlocking the Power of Simplicity in Writing

In the world of writing, complexity is often mistakenly equated with depth. However, the truth is that the most impactful narratives are often clear and straightforward. This chapter delves into why embracing simplicity can enhance your writing, making your narratives not only more accessible but also more powerful.

Many writers fall into the trap of overcomplicating their work, perhaps out of fear that simplicity might make their ideas seem trivial. However, *simplicity is not about diminishing your ideas but presenting them clearly and precisely*. By stripping away the unnecessary layers of complexity, you allow the core message to resonate clearly with your audience.

RECOGNIZING THE CLUTTER

The first step toward simplifying your writing is recognizing how excess complexity can obscure your message. Every word and sentence should serve a purpose. If a piece of text does not support your central idea or narrative, it might only muddy the waters for your readers.

Methods for Streamlining Your Writing

Learning to simplify your writing while retaining its depth involves mastering several vital techniques. These include focusing on active voice, avoiding unnecessary jargon, and breaking complex ideas into understandable segments. *Simplification does not strip your work of sophistication but enhances its elegance and effectiveness.*

Practice Makes Perfect

The practical application of these principles is crucial. This chapter will guide you through exercises and examples on how to apply these simplification techniques in various types of writing. Whether you are crafting a short story, an academic piece, or a business report, the ability to convey complex ideas with simplicity is invaluable.

By embracing clarity and engagement as foundational aspects of writing, you'll find that not only does your writing improve, but so does your connection with your audience. After all, what good is a great idea if it's lost in translation? The practice sections in this chapter are designed to help you hone this skill, transforming even the most intricate subjects into clear, compelling narratives.

This approach will help you achieve a delicate balance between depth and accessibility—ensuring that your writing retains its intellectual rigor while being digestible to a broader audience.

Remember, at the heart of powerful writing lies the ability to touch and inspire readers through words that resonate with clarity and truth.

By simplifying our narratives, we do not dilute them; instead, we distill them to their essence—making every word count towards conveying our core message effectively and beautifully.

Complexity in writing can often act as a veil, obscuring the core message intended for the reader. While intricacy might seem synonymous with depth, it can lead to confusion and dilute the impact of the narrative. Embracing simplicity in writing is not about oversimplifying ideas but distilling them to their essence, making them more accessible and compelling. *By simplifying our narratives, we can amplify their power and resonance, ensuring that our message reaches the reader clearly and effectively.*

When we recognize how complexity can hinder communication, we start to appreciate the beauty of simplicity. *Clarity is vital in conveying our thoughts effectively,* ensuring that our words resonate with readers more deeply. Overcomplicating a narrative can create barriers between the writer and the audience, hindering the emotional connection essential for impactful storytelling. *By stripping away unnecessary layers of complexity, we allow the true essence of our message to shine through.*

In recognizing the pitfalls of complexity in writing, we acknowledge that brevity and clarity are not signs of shallowness but rather hallmarks of powerful communication. *Simplicity does not diminish the depth of our ideas; it enhances their impact by making them more digestible and engaging for the reader.*

Through straightforward storytelling, we invite readers into our world, guiding them through our narrative quickly and gracefully.

Simplicity is not about dumbing down our writing but rather about sharpening its focus, ensuring that every word serves a purpose in advancing the narrative. By shedding unnecessary embellishments and convoluted structures, we create a streamlined path for readers to follow, leading them directly to the heart of our story. *In simplifying our writing, we empower our words to resonate more profoundly with those who encounter them,* leaving a lasting impression long after turning the final page.

Let's delve deeper into methods that can help us simplify our writing while retaining its depth and impact.

When it comes to simplifying writing while maintaining depth, several effective methods can be applied. **One powerful technique** is focusing on the core message or idea you want to convey. By identifying the central theme or purpose of your writing, you can streamline your content and eliminate any extraneous information that does not directly contribute to that main point. This approach ensures that your writing remains clear and focused, allowing readers to grasp the essence of your message without getting lost in unnecessary details.

Another strategy for simplifying writing is to use concrete examples and vivid descriptions to illustrate your points. Instead of relying on abstract language or complex explanations, incorporating tangible examples can make your writing more accessible and engaging for readers. By painting a picture with words, you can create a vivid image in the reader's mind, making your ideas easier to understand and remember.

Additionally, employing a straightforward structure can help simplify writing and enhance clarity. Organizing your content into clear sections with logical transitions between them can guide readers through your narrative smoothly. This structured approach makes it easier for readers to follow your train of thought and helps you stay on track with your main argument or story.

Furthermore, paying attention to your language choice is crucial in simplifying writing. Using plain language that is easily understood by a broad audience can significantly enhance the accessibility of your work. Avoiding jargon, complex terminology, and convoluted sentences can make your writing more approachable and relatable, allowing readers to connect with your ideas more effectively.

A practical tip for simplifying writing is to edit ruthlessly. After drafting your content, go back and review it critically, looking for opportunities to trim unnecessary words or phrases. Concise writing is often more powerful and impactful than verbose prose, so aim to convey your message most efficiently.

Finally, seeking feedback from others can be invaluable in simplifying your writing. Sharing your work with trusted colleagues, friends, or mentors can provide fresh perspectives and insights on further streamlining your content. Constructive criticism can help you identify areas where clarity could be improved and guide you in refining your narrative for maximum impact.

In essence, you can effectively simplify your writing while preserving its depth and impact by focusing on clarity, conciseness, concrete examples, structured organization, simple language, ruthless editing, and seeking feedback.

Descriptive Framework: Simplifying Narrative Crafting

Crafting powerful narratives requires a systematic approach that emphasizes simplicity and engagement. The *"Descriptive Framework"* outlined here provides a structured method for writers to streamline their storytelling while maintaining depth and impact. This framework consists of several vital components that work harmoniously to guide writers through simplification without compromising the essence of their narrative.

Distillation of Core Message

The first step in the framework involves distilling complex ideas into their core messages. *Identifying the primary message or theme* of the narrative is crucial, as it serves as the foundation upon which the entire story is built. By focusing on this central message, writers can eliminate extraneous elements that do not directly contribute to or reinforce the core idea. This process helps clarify the purpose of the narrative. It ensures that every aspect of the story serves a specific function.

Trimming Tree Method

The *"Trimming Tree"* method plays a significant role in simplifying narratives. *This technique involves examining each narrative branch* to determine its necessity and contribution to the story. Writing can create a more streamlined and focused narrative by pruning away unnecessary details, subplots, or characters that do not align with the central message. This process helps maintain clarity and coherence while eliminating distractions that may dilute the story's impact.

Narrative Throughline Strategy

The *"Narrative Throughline"* strategy ensures that every narrative aspect aligns with the central message. ***This approach involves evaluating plot points, character development, and themes*** to ensure they tie back to the core theme. Writers may need to rework sections of the story or merge redundant elements to strengthen the connection between different parts of the narrative. By maintaining a cohesive throughline, writers can create a more engaging and impactful story for their audience.

Refining Language for Clarity

Another critical component of the framework is refining language for clarity. ***Advocating for active voice, precise vocabulary,*** and vivid imagery can help convey complex ideas simply and powerfully. By choosing words carefully and crafting descriptive language that enhances rather than detracts from the narrative, writers can ensure that their message resonates with readers on a deeper level. Clear and concise language is critical to keeping readers engaged and focused on the story's core message.

Feedback Mechanisms

Feedback mechanisms are vital for gauging the effectiveness of simplification efforts and identifying areas for further refinement.

Utilizing digital tools, such as readability score tools and human feedback from writing groups or beta readers, can provide valuable insights into how well the narrative communicates its core message. By seeking feedback from multiple sources, writers can gain a more comprehensive understanding of how their story is perceived and make adjustments to enhance its impact.

In conclusion, by following this Descriptive Framework for simplifying narrative crafting, writers can create powerful and engaging stories that resonate with readers on a profound level.

Each component guides writers through streamlining their storytelling while retaining depth and clarity. Embracing simplicity in writing is vital in amplifying the impact of narratives, allowing writers to convey their core messages with clarity and resonance.

The Essence of Clarity: A Step-by-Step Process to Powerful Writing

In the realm of effective communication, less is often more. Our journey in this chapter underscores a pivotal shift from complexity to clarity, demonstrating that *simplifying your narrative does not strip it of its depth but rather enhances its power.* By refining your approach to crafting stories, you elevate your writing and deepen the connection with your audience.

Step 1: Identify and Eliminate Complexity

First, take a moment to analyze your writing for unnecessary complexities. This could be anything from tangled sentence structures to the overuse of technical jargon that might alienate your reader. Simplifying your language helps in making your message more accessible and impactful. Remember, clarity is the gateway to understanding; ensure your readers do not have to navigate a maze to grasp the essence of your ideas.

Step 2: Refine Your Narrative

Next, focus on distilling your narrative. This involves breaking down cumbersome sentences and opting for precise, vivid language that paints a clear picture for your reader. Embrace the power of showing rather than telling; let your descriptions evoke emotions and thoughts. This method retains the depth of your narrative and makes it more engaging and relatable.

Step 3: Sharpen Your Techniques

Finally, refine your writing techniques to prioritize clarity and engagement. Experiment with active voice, strong verbs, and varied sentence structures to keep the reader interested. Each chapter or section should open and close with strong, clear points that anchor readers' attention and guide them through your narrative. Regular feedback from beta readers or writing groups can be invaluable in this phase, providing insights into areas where confusion may still linger.

This step-by-step process is not just about writing with simplicity; it's about *writing with intention*. Each step builds upon the last, ensuring that every element of your story serves a purpose and contributes to a straightforward, compelling narrative. By dedicating time to each phase, typically a few days to a week, depending on the length and complexity of your work, you allow for thoughtful revision and deeper engagement with your text.

As you continue to practice these steps, remember that the goal is not just to write but to write meaningfully. The clarity you bring to your narratives opens a direct channel to your readers' hearts and minds, making every word count. Embrace this journey of simplification, where each step brings clarity to your writing and amplifies the resonance of your narrative voice. In doing so, you transform simple words into powerful stories that linger in the minds and emotions of your readers long after the last page is turned.

Chapter 6: Feedback is Your Friend: Constructive Criticism as a Tool for Refinement

---

Can Constructive Criticism Unveil the True Potential of a Writer's Craft?

Eleanor sat at her old oak desk, the wood scarred with tales of past endeavors, her fingers poised above the keyboard like a conductor at rest before the symphony began. The room was quiet, save for the soft rustling of leaves outside her window—a gentle reminder of the world moving beyond her thoughts. She had just received feedback from her online writing group, a collective of minds she trusted but whose words today seemed sharper than usual.

Her story, a labor of love she had woven over countless nights, had come back marked with suggestions and critiques that stung more than they should. The screen glowed with comments highlighting awkward phrasing, characters lacking depth, and a plot twist that seemed forced. Each point was a pinprick on her confidence.

As she mulled over the comments, Eleanor recalled her early days filled with similar critiques. Back then, each review felt like an assault rather than assistance. Yet those criticisms honed her skills and sharpened her narratives. Was she not now facing another such moment? Could these pointed words be the chisel to refine her story into something more profound?

The aroma of rain began to seep through the open window, mingling with the earthy scent of old books lining her shelves. She rose and walked over to peer outside. Raindrops pattered against the glass in a steady rhythm, each one a tiny echo of her heartbeat. This was another storm to weather.

Turning back to her desk, Eleanor started typing again—revising a sentence here, rethinking a character there—each change small but significant. She imagined her future readers; what would they feel?

Could she lead them through the narrative's twists and turns more deftly? The feedback that once seemed harsh now guided her pen.

In this quiet room where ideas floated like dust motes in the sunlight filtering through rain-washed windows, Eleanor wrestled with every line until they aligned closer to perfection. The process was painstaking but necessary; in this solitude punctuated by occasional car horns and whispers of wind, stories found their proper form.

As the night deepened and shadows grew longer across scattered papers and books around Eleanor's study, one might wonder: how many revisions it takes for raw prose to transform into resonant artistry?

Embrace the Echoes of Improvement

One of the most transformative tools in mastering the art of writing is feedback. Often perceived as daunting, constructive criticism is, in fact, a golden pathway to refinement and excellence in writing.

This chapter delves into how embracing feedback can dramatically enhance your narrative skills, turning initial drafts into polished gems.

Feedback is essential for growth, not just in writing but in any creative endeavor. It serves as a mirror, reflecting the strengths and areas needing improvement that we might overlook in our creations. Opening ourselves to critique allows our work to evolve beyond the limits of our biases and knowledge gaps. This process is crucial for any writer aiming to resonate more deeply with their readers.

SOURCES OF CONSTRUCTIVE Criticism

Identifying where to gather valuable and unbiased feedback is a critical step. While friends and family can offer helpful insights, their familiarity with us might color their opinions. Therefore, exploring platforms like writing groups and online forums and engaging with beta readers who do not have a personal connection can provide more objective perspectives on your work. These sources offer fresh eyes and diverse viewpoints indispensable for refining your narrative.

One of the most challenging aspects of receiving feedback is the separation between personal attachment and professional development. It's natural to feel closely tied to our creations; after all, each word can feel like a part of our psyche poured onto paper.

However, learning to view critiques as opportunities for growth rather than personal attacks is essential for professional advancement. This mindset shift is beneficial and necessary for those serious about enhancing their writing craft.

Integrating Feedback Effectively

Once you've gathered feedback, the next step is integration. This doesn't mean applying every piece of advice verbatim but rather discerning which suggestions align with your vision and which might lead you astray. It's about finding balance and weaving external insights into your narrative without losing your voice—a skill refined with practice and patience.

Moreover, *constructive criticism should be actionable.* Vague comments like *"it's good"* or *"I didn't like it"* are not particularly helpful. Encouraging detailed critiques will provide concrete elements that can be improved or altered. This specificity transforms feedback from mere opinion into a practical tool.

The Emotional Quotient

Handling criticism requires resilience and an understanding heart. Not every critique will be delivered gently, and learning to extract helpful advice from even the harshest comments without taking them to heart requires both courage and emotional intelligence.

Ultimately, this chapter aims to guide you through these nuanced terrains of receiving, processing, and integrating feedback into your writing process effectively. By doing so, you'll find that *feedback is your friend*—a friend who challenges you, pushes you beyond your comfort zone and leads you toward unparalleled mastery in your writing endeavors.

Embracing this approach will refine your skills and broaden your understanding of different perspectives, enhancing your personal growth and professional prowess in the literary world.

Constructive feedback is the cornerstone of growth for any writer. It offers a fresh perspective, illuminating blind spots that we, as authors, might overlook in our own work. Embracing feedback is not a sign of weakness but a testament to our commitment to improvement. *By valuing and integrating constructive criticism into our writing process, we open ourselves to endless possibilities for refinement and growth.*

When we invite feedback, we are inviting others into our creative space. This vulnerability can be intimidating, but it is also liberating.

Feedback helps us see our work through different lenses, offering insights that can elevate our writing to new heights. Through the eyes of others, we can better understand the impact of our words and refine them accordingly.

Constructive criticism is not about tearing down our work but building it up. It gives us the tools needed to chisel away at the rough edges of our writing, revealing the true beauty within.

Embracing feedback means embracing the opportunity to refine our craft, hone our skills, and become better storytellers.

Incorporating feedback into our writing process is a continuous journey toward mastery. *It requires humility, openness, and a willingness to learn from others.* Each critique, each suggestion, is an opportunity for growth and evolution. By valuing feedback as an essential part of our creative process, we pave the way for transformative change in how we approach our writing.

Feedback is not meant to be a hindrance but a stepping stone towards excellence. It propels us forward, guiding us toward a deeper understanding of our craft and pushing us to explore new horizons in storytelling. By integrating constructive criticism into our writing process, we embrace the power of collaboration and community in shaping our narratives.

Continue on this journey of discovery by exploring sources for unbiased and constructive criticism that can elevate your writing further.

Identifying and utilizing sources for unbiased and constructive criticism is pivotal in writing refinement. *Seeking feedback from diverse sources* can provide valuable insights that may not be apparent to the writer alone. *Whether* online or in-person, writing groups offer a platform for exchanging ideas and receiving feedback from fellow writers with different perspectives. *This collaborative environment fosters growth and improvement* by allowing writers to see their work through fresh eyes.

Online forums can also be a valuable resource for obtaining feedback. *Participating in forums dedicated to writing* enables writers to engage with a broader audience and receive varied opinions on their work. *The anonymity of online platforms encourages honest feedback,* leading to more accurate critiques that highlight areas for improvement.

Beta readers, individuals who read a manuscript before publication, are another essential source of feedback. *Choosing beta readers with diverse backgrounds and preference*s can provide a well-rounded perspective on the strengths and weaknesses of the writing. *Their insights can help identify inconsistencies, plot holes, or character development issues* that may have yet to be noticed by the writer.

Professional editors are also valuable resources for constructive criticism. *Their expertise can offer invaluable guidance on structural elements*, grammar, style, and overall writing coherence.

Working with an editor can elevate the quality of the manuscript and refine it to its full potential.

Incorporating feedback from multiple sources allows writers to comprehensively understand their work's strengths and weaknesses. *By embracing criticism as a tool for growth*, writers can refine their craft and enhance the impact of their narratives.

Utilizing various sources of feedback empowers writers to hone their skills and create compelling, engaging stories that resonate with readers on a deeper level.

Receiving constructive criticism allows writers to evolve and elevate their work. *Approaching feedback with an open mind* and a willingness to learn can significantly improve the writing process.

By actively seeking out diverse sources of criticism, writers demonstrate their commitment to growth and refinement in pursuit of mastery in their craft.

Engaging with different perspectives through feedback channels allows writers to develop a more nuanced understanding of their work. *Each critique offers a chance for introspection and refinement*, guiding writers toward greater clarity, coherence, and impact in their storytelling. *Embracing constructive criticism as a vital part of the writing journey* paves the way for continuous improvement and mastery in crafting unforgettable narratives.

Learn to Separate Personal Attachment from Professional Development in Writing

When receiving feedback on your writing, learning how to separate your personal attachment from your professional development is crucial. *This skill is essential for growth and improvement as a writer.* It's natural to feel vulnerable when sharing your work with others. Still, it's important to remember that feedback is not a personal attack—it's an opportunity for growth.

Navigating the Emotions

Receiving constructive criticism can stir up emotions, from defensiveness to self-doubt. *Acknowledging these feelings is the first step towards separating yourself emotionally from your work.* Remember that feedback is meant to help you refine your writing, not tear you down. You can turn critiques into valuable lessons by approaching feedback with an open mind and a willingness to learn.

Focus on Professional Growth

Viewing feedback as a tool for professional development can shift your perspective. Instead of seeing criticism as a reflection of your worth as a writer, see it as a stepping stone towards improvement.

Embrace the opportunity to refine your skills and enhance the quality of your writing. *Every critique, no matter how challenging, has the potential to make you a better writer.*

Embrace Constructive Criticism

Constructive criticism is not an obstacle; it is an invaluable resource. You demonstrate a commitment to honing your craft by welcoming feedback with open arms. Seek out diverse opinions and perspectives to gain a well-rounded understanding of how your work is perceived. Remember that growth often stems from discomfort—embracing constructive criticism can make significant strides in your writing journey.

Separating the Writer from the Work

It's essential to recognize that feedback is directed at your writing, not at you as a person. *By creating this distinction, you can approach critiques with a level-headed mindset.* Separating yourself from your work allows you to evaluate feedback objectively and implement changes without taking things personally. This practice fosters resilience and adaptability in the face of constructive criticism.

Harness Feedback for Progress

Feedback is a powerful tool for writers seeking growth and refinement. *By learning to detach emotionally from critiques,* you can effectively leverage feedback for progress. Embrace each comment as an opportunity to elevate your writing, recognizing that every suggestion contributes to the evolution of your craft.

Transforming feedback into fuel for improvement sets you on a path toward mastery in writing.

Feedback is not merely a tool for improvement; it is the cornerstone of your writing journey, shaping rough drafts into polished masterpieces. Embracing constructive criticism is essential, as it provides unique insights and perspectives that can dramatically enhance your work. By valuing and integrating this feedback, you ensure that your writing resonates more deeply with readers and stands out in its clarity and impact.

Finding reliable sources of unbiased feedback can often be challenging, yet it is vital in refining your craft. Whether through writing groups, online forums, or beta readers, these platforms offer a goldmine of developmental insights that help pinpoint areas for enhancement. Remember, the goal is to strengthen your narrative, and these external perspectives are invaluable for identifying blind spots in your work.

One of the most challenging aspects of receiving feedback is learning to separate personal attachment from the professional development of your writing. It's natural to feel closely tied to your creations. Still, growth comes from viewing constructive criticism as a means to elevate your work, not diminish your effort. This mindset shift is crucial for your evolution as a writer.

By applying these principles, you refine your skills and accelerate your journey toward writing mastery. Each piece of feedback is a stepping stone to more tremendous success, helping you sculpt your words with precision and care. Let each critique guide you, each suggestion inspire you, and each comment motivates you towards becoming the writer you aspire to be.

Embrace this path with resilience and an open heart. The writing journey is filled with challenges, but with the right tools and a receptive mindset, every piece of feedback you receive is an opportunity to learn, grow, and, ultimately, succeed.

Chapter 7: Digital Drafting: The Role of Technology in Modern Writing

Can Technology Truly Enhance the Art of Writing?

The early morning light spilled over the cluttered desk where Thomas sat, surrounded by piles of manuscripts and scribbled notes. His eyes, red from the lack of sleep, scanned the screen where words blinked back at him mockingly. The new software, MovableType.ai, promised to sculpt his scattered thoughts into coherent narratives. Yet doubt gnawed at him as he stared at the digital cursor dancing on the blank page.

Outside, the city was waking up; the distant hum of traffic mingled with sparrows chirping perched on his window ledge. Thomas sipped his coffee—bitter and strong—and remembered his grandfather's old typewriter. How it clacked and chimed with each letter pressed firmly onto paper. It was a rhythmic certainty he missed in this silent digital age.

The tool was supposed to be revolutionary—a writer's closest ally in battling through creative blocks and refining raw drafts into polished gems. As Thomas navigated through its features, adjusting settings that analyzed tone, structure, and style, he wondered if such technology could truly capture the soul of his narrative or if it would strip away its essence under the guise of enhancement.

His phone buzzed a reminder of his meeting with an eager publisher interested in innovative literary voices shaped by technology. The irony didn't escape him. Here he was, struggling to let a machine coax out his voice.

He recalled evenings spent discussing literature with friends who seemed worlds away; their debates about authenticity in writing now echoed in his mind as he interacted with this new artificial mediator. Could a machine understand human emotions well enough to translate them into words that resonate with real people? Or did it merely echo back what it had been fed by countless other users?

Thomas felt relieved and detached as he adjusted his glasses and leaned closer to observe MovableType.ai, suggesting an opening line for his story. The tool did not tire or need inspiration—it worked relentlessly, providing options derived from algorithms that knew nothing of sleepless nights or heartaches that often birthed profound narratives.

The cool breeze from outside carried in scents from the bakery down the street—the sweet aroma mingling with city smells—a reminder of life beyond algorithms and digital screens.

As Thomas continued typing, guided yet distant from what unfolded on his screen, he pondered: could this technological assistance truly elevate writing without losing its human touch?

Embracing the Digital Quill: How Technology is Redefining the Art of Writing

In an era where digital innovation permeates every facet of our lives, it is no surprise that this technological evolution has also touched the craft of writing. Tools like MovableType.ai are not just accessories but have become integral to the modern writer's toolkit.

These tools offer more than mere convenience; they promise a transformation in how we approach the creation and refinement of written content. This chapter delves into how such technologies are reshaping the writing process, enhancing clarity, and ensuring that the narrative's essence is preserved and amplified.

The Streamlined Process of Writing

One of the foremost benefits of integrating technology like MovableType.ai into our writing regimen is the *streamlined efficiency* it introduces. Today's writers are tasked with crafting compelling narratives promptly. Digital tools expedite various stages of writing—from research and organization to drafting and revision—allowing writers to focus more on the creative aspects of their work while leaving the mechanical tasks to be handled by algorithms designed for precision.

Understanding Digital Writing Aids

To fully leverage these tools, one must first understand what they offer and how they can be best utilized. Digital writing aids come with functionalities ranging from grammar correction to style enhancement and even content suggestion algorithms that can inspire new ideas or suggest ways to refine existing ones. They act as a *second pair of eyes*, often catching errors and inconsistencies that a human might overlook, thereby increasing the accuracy and professionalism of the final piece.

Preserving Narrative Essence

Perhaps most crucially, technology helps maintain the integrity and essence of a writer's narrative. In our quest for polished prose, there's a risk of diluting our work's original message or emotional core. Advanced writing tools are designed to enhance expression without overriding the writer's unique voice and vision. They ensure that while the language may be refined, the story's heart remains untouched.

By adopting such technologies, writers enhance their efficiency and elevate the quality of their work. The interaction between human creativity and machine precision creates a synergy that can lead to more prosperous, more impactful writing. This chapter will explore these dynamics further, offering insights into how digital tools can be adapted to various writing styles and needs.

EMPOWERING WRITERS Through Technology

The aim here is not just to adapt to new technologies but to master them so that they may serve our creative purposes. With thoughtful integration, digital tools do not replace traditional skills but *enhance and expand* them. They encourage writers to push boundaries and explore new possibilities in narrative construction.

This exploration into digital drafting does not suggest replacing foundational writing skills but emphasizes augmentation that respects and builds upon traditional techniques. As we move forward in this digital age, embracing these tools can significantly empower us as writers, allowing us to produce work that resonates deeply with our readers while maintaining authenticity and emotional depth.

As we continue this journey through understanding how technology fits into modern writing practices, remember that at its core, writing is an art form shaped by human experience and emotion. Technology is merely a tool that offers significant advantages in terms of efficiency and precision to help writers better articulate their vision with clarity and impact.

Digital tools like MovableType.ai have revolutionized the writing process, offering writers a streamlined approach to refining and transforming their thoughts into polished works. These technological aids are pivotal in enhancing editing efficiency, providing objective assessments, and instilling writers with confidence in completing their projects. By honing in on critical enhancements, these tools enable writers to maintain the essence of their narrative while elevating its expression, ultimately making the journey from draft to masterpiece smoother and more enjoyable.

MovableType.ai stands out as a revolutionary tool that assists writers in pinpointing precise improvements within their work. By cutting through the noise and focusing on core ideas, this digital aid empowers writers to enhance their narratives effectively. This streamlined approach ensures writers can refine their writing while maintaining their original vision. *Identifying and implementing enhancements efficiently is a game-changer for writers seeking to elevate their craft.*

Efficient editing is a crucial aspect of the writing process and tools like MovableType.ai excel in providing writers with the means to refine their work objectively. *By offering specific suggestions for improvement*, these digital aids guide writers toward enhancing their writing in a structured manner. This objective feedback is invaluable in helping writers polish their drafts and elevate them to a professional standard.

Objective assessment is another key feature of digital writing aids such as MovableType.ai. *These tools provide writers with an unbiased evaluation of their work*, highlighting areas for improvement and offering suggestions for refinement. This objective perspective can be precious for writers looking to elevate the quality of their writing and ensure that it resonates with their intended audience.

Confidence in completing a writing project is essential for any writer, and tools like MovableType.ai play a significant role in instilling writers with the assurance needed to see their work through to completion. ***By providing clear guidance and feedback***, these digital aids empower writers to tackle complex writing projects confidently and precisely. The support offered by these tools can make a substantial difference in the writer's journey from the initial draft to the final masterpiece.

Explore how MovableType.ai can revolutionize your writing process and elevate your craft.

Digital writing aids like MovableType.ai offer a range of functionalities that can significantly enhance the writing process.

These tools are designed to streamline the drafting and editing stages, providing writers valuable assistance in refining their work.

By leveraging the capabilities of such technologies, writers can achieve a higher level of precision and efficiency in their writing endeavors.

One key functionality of digital writing aids is *enhancement pinpointing*. These tools help writers identify areas that may require improvement, such as grammar, structure, or clarity. By highlighting these specific points, writers can focus their efforts on enhancing the quality of their writing in a targeted manner.

Efficient editing is another essential feature offered by digital writing aids. These tools can assist writers in revising and polishing their work quickly and effectively. By providing suggestions for corrections and improvements, these aids enable writers to fine-tune their writing easily, saving time and effort in the editing process.

Digital writing aids facilitate objective assessment. These tools can offer *insightful feedback* on various aspects of writing, helping writers evaluate their work objectively. By receiving constructive criticism and suggestions for improvement, writers can gain valuable perspectives on further enhancing their writing.

Digital writing aids also promote confident completion. By assisting writers in refining their ideas and expressing them clearly, these tools empower writers to *approach the completion* of their work with confidence. The support provided by such technologies can boost writers' self-assurance and encourage them to finalize their projects with a sense of accomplishment.

By effectively utilizing digital writing aids, writers can maintain the essence of their narratives while enhancing their delivery.

These tools enable writers to stay true to their creative vision while improving the overall quality of their writing. With the assistance of technology, writers can navigate the complexities of the writing process with greater ease and produce polished works that resonate with readers.

Framework Description

Integrating technology into modern writing requires a conceptual model focusing on the interaction between the writer, technological tools, and the creative process. This model has three principal components: input, process, and output. Each element plays a crucial role in augmenting different stages of writing, ultimately leading to more productive and fulfilling outcomes.

Input Phase

In the input phase, technology efficiently gathers and organizes ideas, research, and inspiration. *Digital note-taking apps* allow writers to capture thoughts on the go and maintain a centralized repository of ideas. *Cloud storage solutions* ensure easy access to materials from anywhere, promoting seamless workflow and idea cross-pollination. Moreover, *internet-blocking apps* help writers focus by reducing distractions during research and drafting.

Process Phase

The process phase involves utilizing writing-specific software to enhance the drafting and editing processes. *Sophisticated word processors* with real-time editing features enable writers to refine their work as they go along, streamlining the writing process.

Platforms like *MovableType.ai* offer structural and stylistic suggestions, providing valuable feedback to improve the overall quality of the narrative. Virtual workspaces facilitate creativity flow by offering distraction-free environments for focused writing sessions. Additionally, online communities provide networking opportunities, avenues for collaboration, and valuable feedback loops that enrich the writing experience.

Output Phase

Technology plays a significant role in refining, publishing, and sharing final manuscripts in the output phase. Writers can leverage *digital publishing platforms* to reach wider audiences and showcase their work professionally. *SEO tools for blog writers* help optimize content for search engines, increasing visibility and readership. Social media platforms serve as powerful tools for promotional activities, enabling writers to engage with their audience and build a community around their work.

The synergy between writer, creativity, and technology in this conceptual model highlights how digital tools can support and enhance each phase of the writing journey. By leveraging technology effectively across input, process, and output stages, writers can achieve greater efficiency, creativity, and success in their writing endeavors.

Integrating digital tools like MovableType.ai into the writing process marks a transformative era for writers. These tools are not just about simplifying the mechanical aspects of writing; they are about enhancing the creative flow, ensuring that each word we choose and every narrative we craft resonates deeply with our intended audience. By utilizing such technologies, we can efficiently and precisely refine our ideas into polished narratives.

MovableType.ai stands out by offering functionalities that streamline the cumbersome editing process, allowing us to focus more on the art of storytelling. This is particularly invaluable as it aids in maintaining the authenticity and emotional depth of our narratives, ensuring that the heart of the story is not lost amidst the technicalities of grammar and style corrections.

Moreover, these digital aids provide us with objective assessments of our work. This kind of feedback is crucial as it offers a perspective outside our subjective view, thus helping us identify areas for improvement that we might have overlooked. It's like having a trusted advisor who guides us through refining our drafts into compelling literature.

The beauty of incorporating technology into our writing regimen is that it respects and maintains the narrative's essence. It does not strip away the writer's unique voice but instead enhances the delivery of their stories to the audience. This alignment ensures that the soul of the narrative shines through, supported by a robust structure and clear expression.

As we continue to explore and utilize these technological advancements, we find that they do more than aid in crafting well-polished stories; they empower us to be better storytellers. Each tool offers a stepping stone towards mastering the art of writing, encouraging us to push boundaries and explore new creative realms without the burden of tedious processes.

In embracing these digital tools, we're not just keeping up with the times; we're actively enhancing our ability to tell stories that connect, resonate, and stay with our readers long after they've turned the last page. The journey from a rough draft to a masterpiece becomes smoother and more enjoyable.

Through technology, we gain efficiency and a deeper insight into the craft of writing. Let us continue to leverage these tools to sculpt well-crafted and profoundly impactful narratives. After all, at the heart of excellent writing is the power to move people—and with these technological aids, we are better equipped to do just that.

Chapter 8: The Heart of the Matter: Keeping Your Core Idea Front and Center

---

Can Clarity of Purpose Truly Liberate a Writer?

Eleanor sat by the window, the morning light casting long shadows across her desk cluttered with notes and drafts. She tapped her pen against the notepad, each taps a metronome to her racing thoughts.

The novel she was working on had sprawled out of control, a wild growth of subplots and tangential characters that strayed far from its core. Today, she needed to prune it to find its heart again.

Outside, a sparrow flitted from branch to branch in the budding maple tree, seemingly without effort or doubt. Eleanor watched it for a moment, envying its simplicity. Her mind wandered back to her college days when Professor Ames had lectured on the importance of maintaining a sharp focus in writing. *"A story should be a straight arrow,"* he'd said, *"not a scatter of buckshot."* She had agreed then; she needed that clarity now more than ever.

She sifted through her manuscript pages, her fingers brushing against the rough paper as if hoping to feel where it had all gone wrong. The main character, Lucy, had started strong—a woman grappling with loss and redemption—but now she seemed lost in endless reflections that led nowhere. Eleanor sighed and looked back outside; the sparrow had settled into building its nest.

A knock at the door pulled her from her reverie. It was Jonah, her neighbor and confidant in all things literary. He carried two cups of coffee and an expression mixed with concern and curiosity.

"*Still wrestling with Lucy?*" he asked as he set down the coffee.

"*Yes,*" Eleanor admitted, pushing aside some papers to make room for him at the table. "*I'm trying to strip away what doesn't serve the core idea, but finding that core feels like chasing shadows.*"

Jonah sipped his coffee thoughtfully before responding. "*Maybe you're looking too hard for something already clear in your mind but muddled on paper. Focus on what drew you to tell this story in the first place.*"

Eleanor nodded slowly; his words struck something deep within her—a spark not felt in weeks. They spent hours discussing each chapter's intent and impact, stripping layers until Lucy's journey was clear and compelling.

As dusk crept into the room, Eleanor felt lighter than she had in months. There was work yet to be done, but now she was guided by renewed purpose.

Could this renewed focus be enough for Eleanor's story to resonate deeply with its readers?

Why Clarity is King in Masterful Writing

When crafting compelling narratives, the allure of intricate plots and elaborate language can often sidetrack even the most experienced writers. However, the true essence of powerful writing lies in its clarity and focus. **Maintaining a sharp focus on your core idea** is not merely a stylistic choice; it's a strategic approach that enhances productivity and ensures your message resonates clearly and forcefully with your audience.

A clearly defined core idea is at the heart of every memorable piece of writing. This chapter delves into why keeping this core idea front and center is crucial and how it can transform your writing process. By anchoring your work to a central theme, you prevent the common pitfalls of over-complication and unnecessary diversions, steering clear of clutter that can dilute the potency of your message.

The Power of Focus

Understanding how to focus on the core idea throughout your writing process is fundamental. This approach acts as a guiding beacon, ensuring that every paragraph, sentence, and word serves a purpose. This disciplined approach to writing does more than streamline your work; it amplifies the impact of your narrative, making each element in your story or argument build towards a cohesive whole.

Sidestepping Pitfalls

Distractions abound in the writing process, from the seductive pull of tangential ideas to the allure of complex stylistic flourishes. You will develop skills to recognize and understand how to avoid these distractions. This chapter will explore common detours many writers face and provide practical strategies to stay on track.

Aligning Your Elements

Every part of your writing, from structure to tone to character development *(in fiction)* or argument progression *(in nonfiction)*, must align with and enhance your central message. This alignment ensures your audience remains engaged and absorbs your intended message without confusion or distraction.

This introductory exploration sets the stage for a deeper understanding of how focusing on your core idea can liberate you from the constraints of overthinking and overwriting. It invites you to adopt a more intentional approach to your craft, prioritizing clarity over complexity. As we navigate these concepts together, remember that every piece of advice aims to refine your skills and elevate your writing from good to unforgettable.

By embracing these principles, you not only enhance your ability to communicate effectively but also increase the emotional impact of your work. Whether you're penning a novel, drafting an article, or crafting a business report, the techniques discussed here will help you deliver powerful, clear, and compelling messages.

This chapter promises to inform and transform your approach to writing by realigning your practices around the cornerstone of clarity. Let's embark on this journey together, fostering a deeper connection with our thoughts and readers through masterful simplicity.

Throughout the writing process, it is crucial to maintain a laser focus on the core idea that drives your narrative. By identifying techniques that help you stay centered on this central theme, you can avoid getting lost in unnecessary details and ensure that your message remains clear and impactful. One effective technique is to **create a central thesis statement** that encapsulates the core idea of your piece. This statement acts as a guiding light, steering your writing in the right direction and preventing you from straying off course.

Another helpful strategy is outlining your key points before writing. This roadmap can keep you on track and prevent you from meandering into tangents that detract from your core idea. By having a clear structure in place, you can maintain focus and coherence throughout your piece, ensuring that every paragraph reinforces your central message.

Setting specific writing goals can also help you stay on target. Whether you complete a certain number of words per day or devote a particular amount of time to writing, establishing these milestones can keep you accountable and prevent distractions from derailing your progress. Regularly *revisiting your core idea* as you write can help you realign your focus if you veer off track.

While it's natural for ideas to evolve during the writing process, it's essential to *continuously evaluate whether these changes enhance or detract from your core message*. If new elements enrich your narrative and strengthen your central idea, incorporate them thoughtfully. However, if they risk diluting or overshadowing your core concept, consider setting them aside for another project.

By honing in on techniques that maintain focus on your core idea, you can streamline your writing process and ensure that every word serves a purpose in reinforcing your central message. Remember, clarity and coherence are crucial to engaging readers and leaving a lasting impact on your writing.

Keep reading to discover how to avoid common distractions and stylistic over-indulgences in your writing.

In the writing process, it's crucial to avoid everyday distractions and stylistic overindulgences that can divert your focus from the core idea of your narrative. It's easy to get carried away with elaborate descriptions, intricate metaphors, or excessive details that may dilute the impact of your message. *Maintaining a disciplined approach and avoiding these pitfalls ensures that your central idea remains sharp and compelling throughout your work.*

Distractions come in various forms, from the allure of unnecessary tangents to the temptation of embellishing every sentence with ornate language. While creativity is essential in writing, *overindulging in stylistic flourishes can overshadow the essence of your narrative.* It's vital to strike a balance between creativity and clarity, ensuring that every word enhances your core idea.

One common distraction is the urge to impress rather than express. Writers sometimes prioritize eloquence over authenticity, leading to convoluted sentences and verbose prose that could be clearer to the central message. *Remember that simplicity can often convey ideas more powerfully than complexity.* You can avoid getting lost in unnecessary embellishments by focusing on clarity and conciseness.

Another pitfall to watch out for is losing sight of your central idea amidst a sea of details. While descriptive elements can enrich your writing, excess minutiae can overwhelm readers and detract from the central theme. *Stay vigilant in pruning unnecessary details that do not contribute directly to reinforcing your core message*, allowing your central idea to shine brightly without being overshadowed by superfluous information.

Strive for precision in your writing, cutting through extraneous material to reveal the heart of your narrative. *Every word should serve a purpose,* guiding readers toward a deeper understanding of your core idea. By honing in on the essentials and eliminating distractions, you can create a more impactful and engaging piece that resonates with your audience profoundly.

In navigating the writing process, *resist the allure of stylistic excesses that may dilute the potency of your central idea.* Instead, embrace simplicity and clarity as guiding principles, ensuring that every aspect of your narrative aligns harmoniously to amplify your core message. By steering clear of everyday distractions and focusing on what truly matters, you can sculpt a narrative that captivates and inspires readers with clarity and resonance.

Effectively aligning all elements of writing to strengthen the central message involves a meticulous process that demands attention to detail and a keen eye for coherence. Every word, sentence, paragraph, and section must enhance and reinforce the core idea of the narrative. ***Consistency*** is vital in this endeavor; maintaining a consistent tone, style, and voice throughout the text ensures that the central message remains clear and impactful.

Clarity plays a crucial role in aligning the elements of writing.

Clear and concise language helps convey ideas effectively, preventing ambiguity or confusion that could dilute the central message. By using precise language and avoiding unnecessary complexity, writers can ensure that their message resonates with readers on a deeper level.

Structural organization is another essential aspect of aligning writing elements. ***Logical flow***, smooth transitions between ideas, and a well-defined structure strengthen the central message. Each section should seamlessly connect to the next, leading readers on a coherent journey that reinforces the core idea at every turn.

Supporting details and evidence should also be carefully chosen to complement the central message. ***Relevant examples, anecdotes***, or ***research findings*** can add depth and credibility to the narrative, reinforcing the core idea with solid foundations. However, it's crucial to balance providing sufficient support and avoiding overwhelming readers with excessive details.

Incorporating sensory ***language*** can further enhance the alignment of writing elements. By appealing to readers' senses through vivid descriptions, writers can create a more immersive experience that reinforces the central message on an emotional level. Engaging multiple senses can make the narrative more compelling and memorable, leaving a lasting impression on the audience.

Consistent revision and editing are vital steps in ensuring that all elements of writing are aligned to strengthen the central message.

Through careful review, writers can identify inconsistencies, gaps in logic, or distractions that deviate from the core idea. By refining each element with precision and intention, writers can elevate their work to resonate more powerfully with their audience.

In essence, **aligning all elements of writing to strengthen the central message is about honing every aspect of the narrative towards a singular goal: conveying the core idea effectively.** By meticulously crafting each element with purpose and coherence, writers can create a cohesive and impactful piece that leaves a lasting impression on their readers.

As we wrap up our exploration of maintaining the core idea in your writing, let's reflect on the essential strategies that empower you to craft narratives with clarity and impact. Remember, the essence of excellent writing lies not just in the elegance of its words but in the strength and consistency of its central message.

Identifying techniques to keep your focus is crucial. It's about understanding that every paragraph, every sentence, and every word you write should serve the purpose of your narrative. This disciplined approach ensures that your writing does not stray into tangential areas that dilute the potency of your main message.

Avoiding distractions and stylistic excesses is equally important. It's easy to get carried away with ornate descriptions or complex constructions, especially when you aim to impress. However, simplicity often speaks louder than complexity. Removing these common pitfalls ensures that your writing remains accessible and resonant with your audience.

The alignment of all elements in your writing fortifies your central message. This means that everything in your writing, from your narrative structure to character development, from setting descriptions to dialogues, should echo the core idea. This coherence is what makes a piece of writing not just good but memorable.

Remember, writing is not just about expressing ideas; it's about communicating them effectively. By focusing on your core idea, you channel your creative energies more efficiently and enhance the overall impact of your narrative. This focused approach improves productivity and enriches the reader's experience, making your work truly unforgettable.

Keep your core idea as the compass that guides every element of your writing. It's a beacon that illuminates the path from the first word to the last, ensuring every turn you take enriches and amplifies the central theme. This is how you transform a simple narrative into a compelling saga that captures and holds attention.

Embrace these principles as you move forward. Let them guide you in sculpting words that tell a story, touch hearts, and stir minds. Herein lies the art of masterful

writing—simple, focused, and profoundly resonant.

Chapter 9: The Writing Journey: Cultivating Joy in Creative Expression

Can the Art of Writing Truly Be a Journey of Joy?

Eleanor sat at her old oak desk, which had seen countless seasons change from its place by the window. Outside, leaves whispered secrets to each other as a gentle breeze danced through them, carrying the scent of early autumn with it. The room was quiet except for the soft tap-tap tapping of her fingers on the keyboard.

She paused, her eyes drifting from the screen to gaze at the golden hues painting the landscape.

In her mind, she revisited an earlier conversation with her mentor. This seasoned writer spoke of writing not as a task but as an exploration. Each word paved a path to undiscovered terrains of thought and emotion during this journey. This idea had intrigued Eleanor deeply but also left her restless. Her writing felt more like forging through thick brambles than strolling through lush meadows.

The cursor on her screen blinked steadily, like a heartbeat waiting for direction. She remembered her mentor's words about integrating digital tools and strategies to make writing enjoyable.

Could she transform her approach to see her writing not as a duty to be completed but as an adventure to be cherished?

A sudden gust rattled the windowpane, pulling her back from her reverie. She noticed a robin alight on the sill, tilting its head curiously as if pondering why anyone would stay indoors on such a crisp day. Eleanor smiled faintly; even nature seemed to coax her toward finding joy in every little moment.

Turning back to her computer, she decided to experiment with new software that promised to help organize thoughts and simplify editing processes—perhaps this was what she needed to rejuvenate her love for crafting stories. As she downloaded the tool, she felt excited about rediscovering writing as an enriching journey.

Her fingers resumed their dance across the keyboard, this time lighter and more hopeful. With each word typed, she sensed herself weaving joy into the narrative tapestry she created. Could changing tools and perspectives turn what once felt like an arduous trek into an exhilarating expedition?

As dusk fell and painted shadows across her notes, Eleanor leaned back in her chair, reveling in this newfound sense of freedom within her craft. Outside, the night began its silent descent over the earth's canopy.

Could every writer hold within themselves the power to transform their relationship with words?

Discover the Joy in Every Word

Writing is often viewed through the lens of labor—a task to be accomplished or a mountain to be climbed. However, it is time we shift our perspective and begin to see writing as a journey, an exploration, not just a destination or a checkbox on our to-do lists. This chapter delves into how embracing the process of writing can transform it from a chore to a source of joy and fulfillment.

Reimagining the Writing Process

Imagine if every time you sat down to write, you embarked on an adventure where each word paved a path to discovery. Every sentence brought you closer to understanding yourself and the world around you. This is more than just a fanciful idea but a practical approach to making your writing journey enjoyable. By shifting our focus from merely achieving an end product to savoring the act of creation, we unlock a more profound connection with our craft.

Practices that Enhance Enjoyment

Integrating practices that improve our skills and enhance our enjoyment of the writing process is crucial. Simple adjustments such as setting a comfortable writing space, choosing projects that ignite our passion, or altering our routine can dramatically change our perception of writing. These practices don't dilute the discipline needed; instead, they enrich the experience, making discipline feel less stringent and more like a natural part of our creative expression.

Building Sustainable Writing Habits

Sustainability in writing comes from habits that support our mental health and creative ambitions. Establishing routines that acknowledge and respect our individual rhythms and cycles can lead us to find a steady stream of inspiration and motivation. This isn't about rigid schedules that strain our creativity but about finding what rhythm works best for us and helps us maintain a consistent output without burning out.

Writing as exploration offers us endless opportunities for growth—intellectual, emotional, and even spiritual. Each piece we write can be seen as one step in an ongoing journey that teaches us about narrative structure or character development, resilience, adaptability, and the beauty of human experience.

Through this approach, *we foster a sustainable writing habit* that brings continuous joy and deep satisfaction. It's about building a relationship with your craft based on respect for the process and excitement for discovery rather than fear of failure or anxiety over deadlines.

By embracing these ideas, writers can rejuvenate their approach to their work. They turn what could be seen as monotonous into something vibrant and alive, something eagerly anticipated rather than dutifully scheduled.

Ultimately, when we view writing through this refreshed lens—*an enriching journey rather than a taxing obligation*—we enhance our ability to produce impactful work and multiply the personal rewards it brings us. This mindset shift isn't just beneficial for professional growth; it nurtures our inner lives, making each word we write resonate with authenticity and joy.

As a writer, it's easy to get caught up in the end goal of completing a piece of work. The pressure to produce a finished product can overshadow the joy of the creation process itself. However, shifting your perspective to see writing as a journey rather than a destination can transform your experience entirely. Instead of focusing solely on the outcome, *embrace the journey* of crafting your thoughts into words, relishing each step.

Viewing writing as a journey opens you up to new possibilities and experiences. Each word you write is a step forward, and each edit is a detour that enriches your understanding. Embrace the twists and turns of the creative process, knowing that every setback is an opportunity for growth. *Allow yourself to enjoy the act of writing*, not just the finished piece that results from it.

Approaching writing as a journey also allows you to savor the small victories along the way. Celebrate each moment of inspiration, each breakthrough in your narrative. *Find joy in creating*, letting go of perfectionism, and embracing the messy, beautiful process of bringing your ideas to life on the page.

So, how can you shift your perspective and cultivate joy in your writing journey? Read on to discover practical strategies and tools that will transform your creative process into a fulfilling and rewarding experience.

Integrating practices that enhance the writing process can transform it from a daunting task into an enjoyable and fulfilling experience.

One effective practice is setting aside dedicated time for writing each day. Establishing a routine creates a sense of discipline and commitment to your craft. *Consistency breeds familiarity, making writing feel more natural and less intimidating.* Whether it's early mornings before the day begins or late nights when the world is quiet, finding a time that suits your rhythm can significantly boost your productivity and enjoyment of the writing process.

Another valuable practice is engaging in regular brainstorming sessions. This allows you to explore new ideas, perspectives, and creative avenues. *Giving yourself the freedom to brainstorm without judgment* opens doors to innovative approaches and fresh insights. *Brainstorming helps break through mental blocks and encourages a playful exploration of possibilities*, injecting a sense of excitement and discovery into your writing journey.

Embracing the editing process as an essential part of crafting your work is crucial for writing growth. Editing is not about fixing mistakes but about refining and polishing your ideas.

Approach editing with curiosity and a willingness to experiment, knowing that each revision brings you closer to realizing your piece's full potential. *Viewing editing as an opportunity for improvement rather than a chore can make the process more fulfilling.*

Incorporating mindfulness techniques into your writing routine can also enhance your overall experience. Mindfulness can help you stay present and focused during the creative process, allowing you to tap into your intuition and inner voice more effectively. *Practicing mindfulness while writing can deepen your connection to your work and infuse it with authenticity and depth.*

Seeking feedback from trusted peers or mentors can provide valuable insights and encouragement. Sharing your work with others allows you to gain different perspectives and identify areas for growth. Constructive feedback can guide you in honing your craft, while supportive comments can boost your confidence and motivation. Creating a community of fellow writers who understand the challenges and joys of the creative process can enrich your writing journey.

Integrating these practices into your writing routine allows you to cultivate joy in the creative expression process. Each step taken with intentionality and passion brings you closer to realizing your full writing potential. Embrace these practices wholeheartedly, allowing them to infuse your writing journey with fulfillment, satisfaction, and a renewed sense of purpose.

Writing is a craft that thrives on consistency and dedication. To foster a sustainable writing habit that brings continuous joy and satisfaction, it's essential to prioritize regular practice. *Setting aside dedicated time each day* to engage with writing, whether for a few minutes or several hours, can significantly impact one's creative output. This consistent effort helps hone writing skills and cultivates a sense of fulfillment and accomplishment.

Creating a conducive environment for writing is another crucial aspect of nurturing a sustainable writing habit. Find a space that inspires creativity- a cozy corner at home, a bustling café, or a serene park bench. Surround yourself with elements that motivate you to write, such as inspiring quotes, calming music, or essential oils. By curating an environment that resonates with your creative energy, you can enhance your writing experience and make it more enjoyable.

Incorporating rituals or routines into your writing practice can contribute to sustainability. Whether starting each session with a cup of tea, jotting down ideas in a journal before diving into your work, or ending with a reflective walk, these rituals can signal to your brain that it's time to focus and create. Establishing these habits can help streamline the writing process and make it feel more natural and integrated into your daily life.

Seeking accountability and support from fellow writers or mentors can further bolster your writing habit. Joining writing groups, attending workshops, or even sharing your progress with a trusted friend can encourage and motivate you. Knowing that others are invested in your journey can inspire you to stay committed to your writing goals and maintain a sense of joy.

Embracing flexibility in your writing routine is also crucial to sustaining long-term enjoyment. While consistency is essential, allowing for spontaneity and adaptation in your creative practice is equally vital. Some days may call for structured outlining and meticulous editing. In contrast, others may flow better with free-form expression and exploration. Being open to different approaches and adjusting your process can prevent burnout and keep the joy alive in your writing journey.

Celebrating small victories is essential for maintaining enthusiasm and momentum in your writing practice. Whether you've completed a challenging chapter, received positive feedback on a piece, or simply hit your daily word count goal, take the time to acknowledge and appreciate these achievements. Recognizing your progress and successes can fuel your motivation and reinforce the joy you derive from writing.

In conclusion, fostering a sustainable writing habit that brings continuous joy and satisfaction requires commitment, creativity, support, flexibility, and celebration. By integrating these elements into your writing routine, you can cultivate a fulfilling practice that enhances your craft and nourishes your spirit as a writer.

As we reach the end of our exploration of transforming the writing process into a source of joy, reflecting on how this shift in perspective can profoundly impact your approach to creativity is essential. *Writing is not merely about reaching an endpoint*; it is a continuous journey that offers endless opportunities for personal fulfillment and growth.

Embracing the process with enthusiasm and curiosity turns every writing session into an adventure rather than a chore. By integrating practices that enhance enjoyment—such as setting a comfortable writing environment, using tools that streamline the creative process, and allowing yourself the freedom to explore ideas without harsh judgment—you cultivate a more sustainable and pleasurable writing habit.

This approach makes writing more enjoyable and improves the quality of your work. When you write joyfully, your words resonate with authenticity and deeply engage your readers. This authentic connection is what turns good writing into great writing.

Moreover, fostering a sustainable writing habit that continuously brings joy makes you more likely to persist through challenges.

Each obstacle becomes a stepping stone to better skills and deeper insights, reinforcing resilience in your creative endeavors.

Remember, the true reward lies in the journey—the daily discoveries, the honing of your craft, and the personal satisfaction of expressing your thoughts and stories. Let these elements fuel your passion for writing, turning each page you write into a testament to your dedication and love for the craft.

By shifting our focus from destination to journey, we unlock a more fulfilling path that enhances our skills and enriches our lives.

So, take this knowledge forward, apply it diligently, and watch as your writing transforms into a source of endless joy and discovery.

Chapter 10: Breaking Creative Shackles: Unlocking New Writing Possibilities

―――

Can Breaking Creative Barriers Truly Free a Writer?

Eleanor sat at her old wooden desk, its surface cluttered with stacks of unfinished manuscripts and scattered pens. The dim light from the small window cast long shadows across the room, mirroring the doubts that loomed in her mind. She had been wrestling with her latest project for months, each sentence a battle against the invisible forces of self-doubt and rigid formality that seemed to choke her natural voice.

As she tapped a pencil against her chin, Eleanor's thoughts wandered back to a seminar she attended last week about breaking down creative barriers. The speaker talked passionately about using technology to streamline the writing process and focusing on the heart of the narrative to enhance storytelling. She remembered how the room had buzzed with the energy of shared struggles and aspirations.

A sudden gust of wind rattled the window, pulling Eleanor back from her reverie. She glanced outside, where children played under the golden hues of an autumn afternoon, their laughter piercing through her bubble of isolation. It struck her then how much she missed feeling light and unburdened in her writing, how each word used to flow effortlessly when she first began penning stories as a young girl.

Determined, she opened her laptop and started typing, letting each word come out without judging its perfection or placement. With each sentence crafted, she felt a piece of her old self returning; it was as if she was rediscovering her joy in storytelling by silencing her inner critic and embracing simplicity.

The clock ticked unnoticed as Eleanor continued to write, now more fluidly than before. Her story began taking shape around a central theme that resonated deeply with her experiences — overcoming fear and finding one's voice. It was not just about characters in a novel anymore; it was about everyone who felt stifled by their own doubts.

As night fell and the room grew darker, Eleanor paused to stretch.

She looked around at the quiet comfort of her study, filled with books that smelled of musty wisdom and walls that held echoes of countless brainstorming sessions. This room had seen many phases of her life; perhaps it was time it witnessed a rebirth, too.

In this moment of tranquility mixed with accomplishment, one wonders: does breaking free from our self-imposed shackles always lead us back to our true passions?

Are Your Creative Shackles Holding You Back?

Imagine a world where the writing process is as enjoyable and accessible as the stories we yearn to tell. This chapter delves into the transformative journey of breaking free from the constraints that often bind our creative spirits. We can unlock a realm of endless possibilities by identifying and overcoming these barriers, implementing strategic methodologies, and embracing a liberated approach to writing.

The essence of effective writing lies not just in crafting words but in the freedom with which we express our ideas. Many writers struggle with self-doubt, formal constraints, and the overwhelming desire to perfect every detail. These barriers stifle creativity and hinder our ability to communicate genuinely and powerfully. As we reach this penultimate chapter, let's reflect on the core themes of our exploration: refining ideas into polished narratives swiftly and efficiently by focusing on what truly matters—the heart of your narrative.

Identifying Barriers to Creative Freedom

The first step in liberating oneself from creative shackles is recognizing them. Throughout this book, we've explored various dimensions of writing—from harnessing initial ideas to refining them into compelling stories without succumbing to the pitfalls of over-research or stylistic overwhelm. Here, we focus on internal barriers: self-doubt, perfectionism, and undue adherence to formality that can mute a writer's unique voice.

Strategies for More Enjoyable Writing

With barriers identified, the next logical step is to overcome them through practical strategies. This involves integrating tools and techniques that simplify writing while enhancing creativity and enjoyment. Technology plays a crucial role here; tools like MovableType.ai not only streamline operations but also encourage a more spontaneous writing style free from the clutches of excessive formatting or style concerns.

Embracing a Liberated Writing Approach

Finally, embracing a liberated approach to writing can profoundly impact your creative output. This means allowing narratives to flow naturally without the constant critique that every word must be perfect from the first draft. It's about trusting your creative instincts and allowing them to lead your storytelling process.

By addressing these key elements, writers can make their craft more accessible and fulfilling. The joy derived from unhindered expression is palpable—not just for the writer but also for the reader who engages with their work.

As we approach the conclusion of our journey together, it's essential to remember that mastering writing is not solely about adhering to technical perfection but about embracing imperfections as part of your unique narrative voice. Letting go of unnecessary burdens can liberate your writer's voice and unlock astonishing potential—a theme resonant throughout this guide.

This chapter serves as both a capstone and a bridge; it revisits important lessons while setting the stage for continual growth beyond the pages of this book. By now, you are equipped with tools and perspectives that transform obstacles into opportunities for personal and professional growth in writing.

By understanding and applying these insights, you stand at the threshold of mastering and genuinely enjoying the art of writing—ready to sculpt words into stories that resonate deeply and authentically with your audience.

Identifying and overcoming barriers to creative freedom in writing is crucial to unlocking your full potential as a writer. Many aspiring writers feel stifled by self-doubt, fear of judgment, or rigid adherence to formal writing rules. However, understanding these obstacles and working to break free from them can lead to a more fulfilling and enjoyable writing experience.

One familiar barrier writers face is *self-doubt*, which can manifest as a nagging voice questioning the value of their ideas or the quality of their writing. It's essential to recognize that self-doubt is a natural part of the creative process, not an accurate reflection of their abilities. By acknowledging these doubts and *cultivating self-compassion,* you can begin to quiet that critical inner voice and free yourself to explore new possibilities in your writing.

Another obstacle to creative freedom is the *pressure to conform* to established writing norms and styles. While it's essential to understand the basics of grammar and structure, *don't let rigid rules stifle your creativity.* Embrace experimentation and *allow yourself the freedom to write without constraints.* Remember, some of the most groundbreaking literary works were from writers who dared to defy convention.

Moreover, the *fear of imperfection* can also hinder your creative expression. Understand that perfection is an unattainable goal, and *embracing imperfections can* enrich your writing by adding depth and authenticity. Instead of striving for flawlessness, focus on capturing the essence of your ideas and emotions in your writing.

Additionally, the *pressure for immediate success can* be paralyzing for writers. Remember that *writing is a journey*, and mastery takes time and practice. Set realistic goals, celebrate small victories, and *allow yourself room to grow* without expecting perfection.

Embrace the discovery process as you navigate these barriers towards creative liberation.

By recognizing and addressing these common obstacles, you can create a more authentic, enjoyable, and fulfilling writing experience.

Implementing strategies to make writing more accessible and enjoyable is essential for writers looking to break free from creative constraints. *One key strategy* is to embrace technology as a tool rather than a hindrance. Writing software or apps can streamline the writing process, offering features like grammar checks, word suggestions, and organization tools to enhance efficiency and creativity. By incorporating technology wisely, writers can focus more on their narrative and less on technicalities, allowing ideas to flow more freely.

Another effective strategy is to focus clearly on the narrative's heart. By constantly reminding oneself of the core message or theme of the writing piece, writers can stay grounded in their purpose and avoid getting lost in unnecessary details or distractions. This practice keeps the writing cohesive and helps maintain a solid connection with the reader, ensuring that the essence of the story remains authentic and engaging.

Creating a conducive environment for writing is also crucial in making the process more accessible and enjoyable. Whether finding a quiet space, playing inspiring music, or setting specific writing times, establishing a routine that works best for individual creativity can significantly impact the quality of the work produced. A comfortable and inviting environment fosters creativity and allows ideas to flow naturally, leading to a more enjoyable writing experience.

Another valuable strategy is taking regular breaks during the writing process. Stepping away from the work at intervals allows writers to recharge their creative energy, gain fresh perspectives, and prevent burnout. Taking short walks, practicing mindfulness, or simply resting can rejuvenate the mind and help writers approach their work with renewed vigor and enthusiasm.

Seeking feedback from trusted sources can also enhance the accessibility and enjoyment of writing. Constructive criticism from peers, mentors, or beta readers can provide valuable insights into areas for improvement, sparking new ideas and perspectives that can elevate the quality of the writing. Embracing feedback as a learning opportunity rather than a critique can open up new possibilities for growth and development as a writer.

Incorporating mindfulness *techniques* into the writing process can be transformative in making writing more accessible and enjoyable.

Practices such as deep breathing exercises, visualization, or meditation can help writers stay present in the moment, reduce self-doubt and distractions, and effortlessly tap into their creative flow.

By cultivating mindfulness during writing sessions, writers can unlock new levels of focus, inspiration, and clarity in their work.

Overall, by implementing these strategies effectively, writers can confidently and easily navigate creative barriers. Making writing more accessible and enjoyable enhances the craft itself and fosters a deeper connection with one's creativity and storytelling abilities. Embracing these practices opens up a world of possibilities for writers to explore their full potential and create compelling narratives that resonate with themselves and their audience.

By embracing a liberated approach to writing, you unlock the full spectrum of your creative potential. *By shedding the shackles of self-doubt and formal constraints, you pave the way for genuine expression and uninhibited storytelling.* This liberation is about breaking free from rules and delving deep into your inner voice, allowing it to guide your words with authenticity and passion.

Embrace Imperfection: Remember that perfection is often the enemy of creativity. *Allow yourself the freedom to make mistakes, knowing that they are stepping stones toward growth and improvement.* Imperfections can add depth to your writing, making it more relatable and engaging for your audience.

Trust Your Instincts: Your intuition is a powerful tool in writing. *Listen to your inner voice; it knows the heart of your story better than any rulebook.* Trusting your instincts can lead you to unexpected and remarkable places in your narrative, infusing it with a unique essence that sets it apart.

Stay Curious and Open: Maintain a sense of curiosity and openness in your writing process. *Explore new ideas, experiment with different styles, and be willing to take creative risks.* This openness can lead you to discover innovative approaches that breathe fresh life into your work.

Find Joy in the Process: Writing should be a source of joy and fulfillment. *Celebrate small victories along the way, relish in moments of inspiration, and savor the act of creation.* Writing becomes a rewarding journey rather than a daunting task when you find joy in the process.

Connect with Your Audience: Remember that writing is a form of communication. *Write with empathy, seeking to connect with your readers personally.* You create a profound bond that elevates your storytelling by weaving narratives that resonate with their emotions and experiences.

Celebrate Your Uniqueness: Your voice is unlike any other. *Celebrate your uniqueness by embracing what sets you apart as a writer.* Honor your individuality and use it as a powerful tool to craft authentic, compelling, and wholly your narratives.

Persist in Your Pursuit: Writing is a journey of ups and downs. *In moments of doubt or struggle, remember that resilience is critical.* Persist in your pursuit of creative expression, drawing strength from challenges and setbacks as fuel for growth and transformation.

Harnessing a liberated approach to writing taps into an endless wellspring of creativity within yourself. *By unlocking this potential, you not only enrich your writing experience but also offer readers vibrant, authentic, and resonant narratives.* Trust in the power of liberation to set free the true essence of your storytelling craft.

As we reach the final pages of our exploration into the art of writing, it's essential to reflect on the transformative journey we've embarked upon. We've dissected the intricacies of breaking through creative barriers, making writing not only more accessible but also a delightful pursuit. This final chapter has underscored the importance of liberating oneself from self-doubt and rigid formalities often stifling creativity.

Identifying and overcoming barriers to creative freedom has been a cornerstone of our discussions. Acknowledging and addressing these obstacles has opened up new avenues for expression and innovation in our writing. The strategies implemented to make writing more accessible have, undoubtedly, lightened the load, allowing ideas to flow more freely and with greater clarity.

Moreover, the concept of a ***liberated writing approach*** has been about technique and embracing a mindset. When writers release themselves from unnecessary constraints, they tap into a wellspring of authentic and powerful creativity. This authenticity breathes life into words and transforms simple narratives into resonant stories that linger in readers' minds and hearts.

Throughout this book, we've tackled the overwhelming struggle many face—perfecting unique ideas without getting lost in the minutiae of excessive research or stylistic concerns. By focusing on refining these ideas into polished masterpieces, writers can achieve remarkable progress in weeks, not years.

The tools and strategies discussed, from leveraging technology like MovableType.ai to maintaining a laser focus on the heart of the narrative, are more than just techniques; they are pathways to rediscovering the joy and fulfillment that writing should bring. This approach not only makes writing more accessible but also enhances the writer's ability to connect with their audience on a deeper level.

Let us carry forward this spirit of *unencumbered creativity*. Let every word we write be a step towards mastering the art of storytelling. As you continue to write, remember that each page you fill is not just about crafting words but about sculpting ideas that have the power to move, persuade, and transform.

By embracing these principles, you are equipped to overcome challenges and excel in your writing endeavors. The journey does not end here; it evolves with every story you tell. Write boldly, write freely, and let your unique voice shine through every sentence you craft.

Epilogue

Embracing Your Mastery: The Journey Continues

As we conclude this journey together, reflecting on the transformative path you've embarked upon is essential. The essence of writing is not just creating words but *sculpting thoughts* that resonate deeply with your audience. This book aims to equip you with the tools and strategies necessary to refine your ideas into narratives that not only capture attention but also withstand the test of time.

These strategies have vast and varied real-world applications.

Whether you're drafting a novel, crafting articles, or penning scripts, focusing on core ideas and minimizing distractions apply universally. Implementing these techniques in your daily writing practice can dramatically enhance your productivity and creativity.

We revisited several vital concepts throughout this book:

- *Streamlining research* to avoid getting lost in a sea of information.
- Emphasizing *clarity and precision* in your writing to enhance readability and impact.
- Tools like MovableType.ai can *break down creative barriers*, making the process more accessible and enjoyable.

To truly benefit from these insights, apply them consistently. Start small, perhaps with a short story or a blog post, using the streamlined approach we've discussed. As you grow more comfortable, expand these practices into larger projects.

It's important to acknowledge that no guide can cover every aspect of an art as intricate as writing. There may be moments when you find yourself facing new challenges that were not addressed in these pages. In such times, remember that further exploration and continuous learning are part of your growth as a writer.

Armed with knowledge and strategies, it's time for you to take action. Let each word you write reflect your newfound clarity and focus. Let each narrative you craft be imbued with passion and precision.

Remember, the beauty of writing lies in its ability to evolve—as do its craftsmen. Keep refining your skills, exploring new horizons, and pushing beyond boundaries. Your journey as a masterful writer does not end here; it evolves with every word you sculpt.

In closing, let me leave you with a thought from one of the greatest storytellers, William Shakespeare:

"The object of art is to give life a shape."

May the shape you give your art be as profound and impactful as it is unique. Here's to your continued success on this incredible journey of crafting unforgettable narratives.

Don't miss out!

Visit the website below and you can sign up to receive emails whenever Perry L. Davidson publishes a new book. There's no charge and no obligation.

https://books2read.com/r/B-A-UIWNB-HMDHF

BOOKS 2 READ

Connecting independent readers to independent writers.

Also by Perry L. Davidson

Charisma Unlocked: Forge Lasting Bonds and Radiate Influence
Unleashing the Power of Likability and Charisma
The Stoic Compass: Charting a Course to Serenity in the Modern Age
The Eternal Ink: Keeping the Writer's Flame Alive
Unshakeable: The Stoic's Path to Inner Strength and Serenity
Embrace Your Emotions: Mastering Emotional Intelligence for a Harmonious Life
Fandom Unveiled: Harnessing the Heartbeat of Sports Loyalties
Community Craft: The Art of Building Engaged Digital Spaces
Speaking Hearts: Unlocking the Power of Parent-Child Conversations
Sculpting Words: Carving Your Path to Masterful Writing
Sculpting Words: Carving Your Path to Masterful Writing

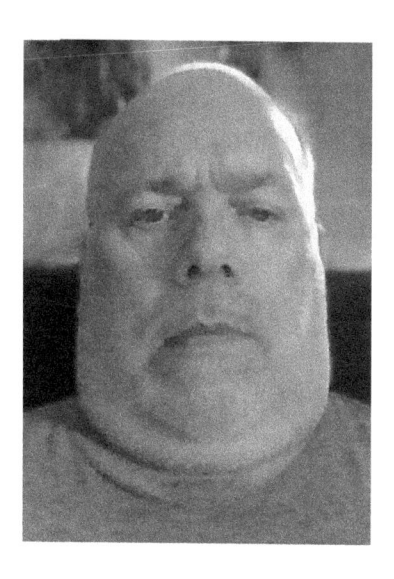

About the Author

At age 67, Perry L. Davidson is embarking on a journey that intertwines the culmination of a lifetime's experiences with fulfilling a long-held dream: publishing his first book. As a Navy veteran and a retired dispatcher, Perry L. Davidson brings a wealth of life experiences to his writing, which is marked by years of service, dedication, and a deep understanding of the human spirit.

Born and raised in Charleston, South Carolina, Perry L. Davidson spent his early years absorbing the stories and landscapes that would later become the backdrop for his narratives. His time in the Navy not only instilled in him a sense of discipline and resilience but also exposed him to a diversity of people and places, enriching his perspective and deepening his appreciation for the myriad ways in which life unfolds.

After his service, Perry L. Davidson transitioned to a career as a dispatcher. This role sharpened his ability to listen, empathize, and communicate effectively under pressure. These years were not just about managing crises but about understanding the stories behind each call. This experience honed his storytelling skills and fueled his passion for writing.

Now, in retirement, Perry L. Davidson has turned to the pen (or keyboard) as his tool for exploration and expression. His writing is a testament to his belief in the power of stories to connect, heal, and inspire. The themes of courage, perseverance, and the search for meaning that run through his work reflect his own life's journey.

Publishing his first book is a personal achievement for Perry L. Davidson and a gift to his readers. It offers insights and inspirations drawn from a well-lived life. As he steps into literature, he hopes to encourage others, regardless of age, to pursue their dreams and tell their stories, proving that it's always possible to start a new chapter.